A GLOSSARY OF SOCIOLINGUISTICS

A Glossary
of Sociolinguistics

Peter Trudgill

OXFORD
UNIVERSITY PRESS

Oxford University Press

Oxford New York

Auckland Bangkok Buenos Aires Cape Town Chennai

Dar es Salaam Delhi Hong Kong Istanbul Karachi Kolkata

Kuala Lumpur Madrid Melbourne Mexico City Mumbai Nairobi

Sao Paulo Shanghai Singapore Taipei Tokyo Toronto

Published by Oxford University Press, Inc.
198 Madison Avenue, New York, New York 10016
by arrangement with Edinburgh University Press Ltd
22 George Square, Edinburgh, United Kingdom

Oxford is a registered trademark of Oxford University Press, Inc.

Typeset in Sabon by Hewer Text Ltd, Edinburgh

Printed and bound in Great Britain by
Cox & Wyman Ltd, Reading, UK

Library of Congress Cataloging-in-Publication Data

Trudgill, Peter.
    A glossary of sociolinguistics / Peter Trudgill.
        p.cm.
    Includes bibliographical references.
    ISBN 0-19-521943-0
        1. Sociolinguistics–Terminology. I. Title.

 P40 .T747 2002
 306.44'01'4–dc21

                                        2002038174

Introduction

The aim of this book is to provide an introductory guide to the central concepts and most frequently used technical terms used in sociolinguistics. The focus is not only on the various branches of sociolinguistics itself, but also on dialectology, both traditional and modern, and on varieties of the English language, particularly those which have been of especial interest to people working in sociolinguistics. Classic studies in sociolinguistics are also cited. There is, too, a particular emphasis on individual languages of types which tend to be of special interest to sociolinguists, such as minority languages, and pidgin and creole languages.

The entries are written in normal prose, but are presented alphabetically to facilitate research, and with numerous cross-references. The book is a revised, updated and much expanded version of the author's *Introducing language and society* (Penguin, 1992).

Acknowledgements

I am very grateful to the following for their help and advice in the preparation of this book: Jenny Cheshire, David Crystal, Yvonne Dröschel, Mercedes Durham, Jan Terje Faarlund, Jean Hannah, Daniel Long, Didier Maillat, James Milroy and Lesley Milroy.

Aasen, Ivar see **Ausbau language, Nynorsk**

AAVE see **African American Vernacular English**

Abstand language (German /ˈapʃtant/) A concept developed by the German sociolinguist Heinz Kloss. A variety of language which is regarded as a **language** in its own right, rather than a **dialect**, by virtue of being very different in its linguistic characteristics from all other languages. The degree of linguistic distance (German 'Abstand') between this variety and other languages is such that, unlike **Ausbau languages**, there can be no dispute as to its language status. Basque, the language spoken in northern Spain and southwestern France, is a good example of an Abstand language. It is clearly a single language, because its dialects are similar. And it is clearly a language rather than a dialect because, since it is not related historically to any other European language, it is completely different in its grammar, vocabulary and pronunciation from the neighbouring languages, French and Spanish – compare the numerals from *one* to *five*.

French	Spanish	Basque
un	*uno*	*bat*

deux	*dos*	*bi*
trois	*tres*	*hiru*
quatre	*cuatro*	*lau*
cinq	*cinco*	*bost*

The Basque-speaking area

There is no widely used English equivalent for this term, but 'language by distance' is sometimes employed.

accent The way in which people pronounce when they speak. Since everybody pronounces when they speak – everyone has phonetics and phonology – everybody speaks with an accent. A speaker's accent may relate to where they are from geographically (for example a London accent, an American accent – see also **Geordie, Scouse, Cockney**). It may relate to their social background (for example an upper-class accent, or, in England, an **RP** accent) or it may relate to whether they are a native speaker or not (for example a French accent, a foreign accent). Accent and **dialect** normally go together (Yorkshire dialect is spoken with a Yorkshire accent) but British sociolinguists distinguish between the two because the **RP** accent and the **Standard English** dialect are not always combined.

accommodation The process whereby participants in a conversation adjust their **accent, dialect** or other language characteristics according to the language of the other participant(s). Accommodation theory, as developed by the British social psychologist of language, Howard Giles, stresses that accommodation can take one of two major forms: convergence, when speakers modify their accent or dialect, etc. to make them resemble more closely those of the people they are speaking to; and, less usually, divergence, when, in order to signal social distance or disapproval, speakers make their language more unlike that of their interlocutors. Accommodation normally takes place during **face-to-face interaction**.

accountability, principle of A principle propounded by William Labov which states that reports of the occurrence of a variant of a **linguistic variable** must be accompanied by reports of its non-occurrence.

acrolect A **variety** or **lect** which is socially the highest, most prestigious variety in a social **dialect continuum**. Other varieties lower down the social dialect continuum in terms of social status are known as **mesolects** and **basilects**. This terminology is particularly common in the discussion of the sociolinguistic situation in **post-creole continuum** communities such as Jamaica, where **Standard English** is the acrolect, Jamaican **Creole** the basilect, and linguistically intermediate varieties the mesolects.

act of identity According to the British sociolinguist Robert LePage, any **speech act** performed by an individual is an act of identity. In any given situation, speakers will select from the range of **varieties** available to them in their **verbal repertoires** depending on which personal and social identity they wish to project. By selecting a pronunciation or grammatical form or word associated with and symbolic of a particular group in society, they will be projecting their identity as a member of that social group rather than some other identity. **Accommodation** of both the convergence and divergence types can be interpreted as constituting an act of identity.

actuation problem One of a number of problems pointed to by the American sociolinguist William Labov in connection with the study of linguistic change within the field of **secular linguistics**. The actuation problem is the problem which linguists have of explaining why a particular linguistic change is set in motion in the first place. Historical linguists may be quite good at accounting for particular sound changes or grammatical changes, but why do changes start where and when they do, and not at some other place or time? A related problem, as discussed by Labov, is the **embedding problem**.

address forms Words and phrases used to address other people in conversations, meetings, letters, etc. Address forms may include pronouns such as *you*, titles such as *Sir* and *Madam*, names such as *John* and *Mr Smith*, and endearments and expressions such as *mate*, *buddy*, *dear*, *honey*. In all communities, there are norms concerning who uses which form to who, what the social implications are of using one form or another, and on which occasions particular forms may be used. In Britain, it would be unusual to address a friend by title plus surname, for example *Mr Smith*, and more usual to address them by their first name, for example *John*. In many languages, speakers also have to select second-person pronouns, corresponding to English *you*, according to sociolinguistically appropriate norms. Selection usually involves a choice of **T and V pronouns**.

adjacency pair In **conversation analysis**, a sequence of two utterances by two different speakers in which the second is related to the first in a specific way. For example, a question will normally be followed by an answer, and a summons by a response, as in:

A: Mum!
B: Coming!

admixture The mixing of elements from one language or dialect into another. This typically happens when speakers are using a variety that is not their native tongue and interference, such as the use of a foreign accent or the transfer of grammatical patterns from one language to another, takes place. Admixture is an important notion in the study of **pidgin** languages and is one of the major elements in the process of **pidginisation**. Admixture can also involve the **borrowing** of words from one language to another.

adstratum see **substratum**

African American Vernacular English (AAVE) The name used by American sociolinguists to refer to the **dialect** of English spoken, with relatively little regional variation, by lower-class anglophone (i.e. not Louisiana French Creole-speaking) African Americans in the United States. In its phonological and, especially, grammatical characteristics (such as **copula deletion**), this **variety** differs from White dialects of English in such a way that many linguists have argued that it represents a late stage historically in a **decreolisation** process of an earlier **creole** that formerly resembled the creoles of the Caribbean and **Gullah**. Other linguists, sometimes known as 'anglicists', argue that the linguistic features of AAVE can be entirely accounted for by an origin in the British Isles. William Labov has argued, in research published in the 1980s, that African American Vernacular English is currently diverging from White dialects. This research has led to the **divergence controversy** in American sociolinguistics. AAVE has also been called '**Ebonics**'.

Afro-Seminole see **Gullah**

age-grading A phenomenon in which speakers in a community gradually alter their speech habits as they get older, and where this change is repeated in every generation. It has been shown, for example, that in some speech communities it is normal for speakers to modify their language in the direction of the **acrolect** as they approach middle-age, and then to revert to less prestigious speech patterns after they reach retirement age. Age-grading is something that has to be checked for in **apparent-time studies** of linguistic change to ensure that false conclusions are not being drawn from linguistic differences between generations.

Americana At the end of the American Civil War in 1865, thousands of Americans from the defeated South left the United States and about 40,000 of them went to Brazil where they founded a number of settlements. The best known of these is called Americana, which is about 100 miles northwest of Sao Paulo. The language of the community was for many decades a Southern variety of American English, and there are many hundreds of older people today who still speak a conservative form of English which has its roots in Georgia and Alabama. Gradually the community have become bilingual in English and Portuguese, and **language shift** to Portuguese is now taking place.

anglicists see **African American Vernacular English**

Angloromany The ethnic language of the Rom (Gypsies) is Romani, an originally North Indian language related to Hindi and Panjabi. As a result of **language shift,** however, Gypsies in England no longer speak the language. Many of them, though, are still able to speak a variety known as Angloromany or Anglo-Romany. This is a variety in which, as described by the British Gypsy linguist Ian Hancock, many of the nouns, verbs and adjectives are of Romany origin, while the articles, numerals, conjunctions, pronouns, prepositions and grammatical endings, as well as the phonetics and phonology, are English. Angloromany may function as an **antilanguage** and it has provided important input in the development of English **slang**. Here is an example:

> Jesus pukkered them this parable. 'Suppose tutti's got a hundred bokros and yek of them's nasherdi. Is there a mush among the lot of you as would not muk the ninety-nine in the bokro-puv and jel after the nasherdi bokro till he latchers it? Karna he's latchered it he riggers it on his dummer, well-pleased he is. Karna he jels home he pukkers his friends and all the foki around "Be happy with mandi, because I've found my nasherdi bokro".'

Jesus told them this parable. 'Suppose you've got a hundred sheep and one of them's lost. Is there a man among the lot of you who would not leave the ninety-nine in the sheepfold and go after the lost sheep till he finds it? When he's found it he lays it on his shoulder, well-pleased he is. When he gets home he tells his friends and all the neighbours aound "Be happy with me, because I've found my lost sheep".'

Ann Arbor case A court case in the town of Ann Arbor, Michigan, USA, in 1979, in which African American parents argued that insufficient provision had been made in the education system for children who were native speakers of **African American Vernacular English** rather than **Standard English**. William Labov presented evidence showing that African American Vernacular English was a systematic, rule-governed linguistic variety. The court ruled that the education system should take account of the fact that children came to school speaking a structured language variety which is linguistically different from Standard English. See **linguistic gratuity, principle of**.

anthrolinguistics see **anthropological linguistics**

anthropological linguistics A branch of the study of language and society, sometimes known as anthrolinguistics, in which the objectives of the study are in part identical to those of anthropologists – to find out more about the social structure of particular communities (especially but not exclusively in smaller non-European societies) – but where the methodology involves analysis of languages and of norms for language use. Areas studied in anthropological linguistics include **kinship terminology**, the **Sapir-Whorf hypothesis** and linguistic **taboo**. There are also strong connections between anthropological linguistics and the **ethnography of speaking**.

antilanguage A term coined by Michael Halliday to refer to a variety of a language, usually spoken on particular occasions by members of certain relatively powerless or marginal groups in a society, which is intended to be incomprehensible to other speakers of the language or otherwise to exclude them. Examples of groups employing forms of antilanguage include criminals, drug-users, schoolchildren, homosexuals and Gypsies. Exclusivity is maintained through the use of **slang** vocabulary, sometimes known as **argot**, not known to other groups, including vocabulary derived from other languages. European examples include the antilanguages **Polari** and **Angloromany**. Some of these varieties rely on phonological or other distortion processes to make them incomprehensible – see **back slang**, **Pig Latin**, **rhyming slang** and also **gayspeak**.

Appalachians, the A hilly area of the eastern United States which has been much studied by American dialectologists because of its **traditional dialects**. The areas of most interest to dialectologists have been in West Virginia.

apparent-time studies Studies of linguistic change which attempt to investigate language changes as they happen, not in real time (see **real-time studies**), but by comparing the speech of older speakers with that of younger speakers in a given community, and assuming that differences between them are due to changes currently taking place within the dialect of that community, with older speakers using older forms and younger speakers using newer forms. As pointed out by William Labov, who introduced both the term and the technique, it is important to be able to distinguish in this comparison of age-groups between ongoing language changes and differences that are due to **age-grading**.

applied linguistics The application of the findings of linguistics to the solution of real-world problems. The term is most often used in connection with the application of linguistics to the teaching of foreign and second languages.

applied sociolinguistics The application of the findings of sociolinguistics to the solution of real-world problems. See **Ann Arbor case, cross-cultural communication, interactional sociolinguistics, language conflict, language cultivation, language planning, language revival, verbal deprivation**.

areal linguistics see **geographical linguistics**

argot /argou/ A term sometimes used to refer to the kinds of **antilanguage** whose **slang** vocabulary is typically associated with criminal groups.

artificial languages see **historicity**

Arumanian see **Vlach**

Arvanitika The name given in Greece to the language of the indigenous Albanian-speaking **linguistic minority** in that country. This minority has been in Greece since medieval times, and the biggest concentration today is found in Attica, Biotia and much of the Peloponnese. Many of the suburbs of Athens are, or were until recently, Albanian-speaking. The number of speakers is difficult to determine but there may be as many as 50,000. There is no doubt that Arvanitika is a variety of Albanian – the degree of linguistic **Abstand** between it and the dialects of southern Albania is so small that mutual intelligibility is not difficult. However, the practice of referring to the language by a different name has the effect of implying that Arvanitika is an autonomous language rather than a dialect of Albanian, the national language of a neighbouring country.

audience design A notion developed by Allan Bell to account for **stylistic variation** in language in terms of speakers' responses to audience members i.e. to people who are listening to them. Bell's model derives in part from **accommodation** theory.

augmentative The opposite of **diminutive**. A form, usually of a noun, with the added meaning of 'big'. In European languages this is usually signalled by a suffix, as in Greek *pedharos* 'big boy' from *pedhi* 'child'. There is frequently an additional association of admiration, such that *pedharos* most often means 'big, good-looking lad'.

Ausbau language (German /'ausbau/) A concept due to the German sociolinguist Heinz Kloss. A **variety** which derives its status as a **language**, rather than a **dialect**, not so much from its linguistic characteristics, like an **Abstand language**, but from its social, cultural and political characteristics. These characteristics will normally involve **autonomy** and **standardisation**. Norwegian and Swedish are regarded as distinct languages, not because they are linguistically very different from one another – there is clear **mutual intelligibility** – but because they are associated with two separate, independent nation states, and because they have traditions involving different writing systems, grammar books and dictionaries. **Ausbau** is the

German word for 'extension' or 'building up'. Note that when new Ausbau languages are being developed through **language planning,** planners will often make the most of what Abstand is available. For example, Ivar Aasen, the developer of the form of Standard Norwegian now known as **Nynorsk** deliberately modelled it on those (western) dialects which were least like Danish, which had hitherto been the standard language of Norway. There is no widely used English equivalent for this term, but 'language by extension' is sometimes employed.

Austin, J. L. see **speech act theory**

autonomy A term, associated with the work of the Norwegian-American linguist Einar Haugen, which means independence and is thus the opposite of **heteronomy.** Autonomy is a characteristic of a **variety** of a language that has been subject to **standardisation** and **codification,** and is therefore regarded as having an independent existence. An autonomous variety is one whose speakers and writers are not socially, culturally or educationally dependent on any other variety of that language, and is normally the variety which is used in writing in the community in question. **Standard English** is a **dialect** which has the characteristic of autonomy, whereas **Cockney** does not have this feature.

avoidance language A linguistic variety which is used to permit social interaction between people who would otherwise be prevented from communicating with one another by strong social **taboos.** In many Australian aboriginal communities there are taboos concerning communication between a man and his mother-in-law. In some such communities they are permitted to talk to one another only if they employ a special language variety, sometimes known as a mother-in-law language, in which a special reduced vocabulary is used and sometimes also a different phonological system.

B

back slang A form of **antilanguage** in which words are deliberately disguised by being pronounced backwards, as in *Kool toul!* 'Look out!' and *riah* 'hair'. The British **slang** term *yob* 'uncouth male person' was originally back slang for *boy*.

Ballymacarett see **Belfast**

Bamyili Creole see **Kriol**

basilect In a social **dialect continuum**, the **lect** which has the lowest social status. In the Jamaican **post-creole continuum**, the basilect is the variety most unlike the **Standard English acrolect**, namely Jamaican **Creole**. Ranged above the basilect on the continuum are the **mesolects** and the **acrolect**.

Bay Islands The Bay Islands of Honduras are a group of eight small islands off the northern coast of the mainland of that country. The islands were settled in 1642 by English buccaneers. English-speaking Protestants formed the majority of the population until about 1900, when Hispanic Hondurans from the mainland began settling, but indigenous anglophones still form about eighty-five per cent of the population. See **Central American English**.

Belfast The largest city in Northern Ireland. The three Belfast areas of Ballymacarett, Clonard and The Hammer were investigated by the British linguists James Milroy and

Lesley Milroy in their pioneering sociolinguistic study of that city, some of the results of which were published in L. Milroy *Language and social networks* (2nd edn, 1987) and in J. Milroy *Linguistic variation and change* (1992).

Bell, Allan see **audience design, style axiom**

Belten High The name used by Penelope Eckert to refer to the American High School in Michigan in which she carried out fieldwork on which her two books *Jocks and burnouts: social identity in the high school* (1989) and *Linguistic variation as social practice* (2000) are based. The two main groups of pupils identified by Eckert were the 'jocks', who were those who identified most with school values and who also used more conservative variants of vowels involved in the **Northern Cities Chain Shift**; and 'burnouts', who identified more with the working class and often anti-school values of urban Detroit, and were more innovative in their usage of vowel variants. See also **community of practice**.

Bernstein, Basil see **elaborated code, restricted code**

Bichelamar see **Bislama**

Bickerton, Derek see **bioprogram hypothesis**

bidialectalism (1) The ability of a speaker to command more than one dialect of a language, and to show **code-switching** from one to another depending on **social context**. This ability is more common in **divergent dialect communities**. Most often, bidialectalism involves the ability to use the standard dialect of a language together with some **nonstandard dialect**. (2) An educational policy which is intended to give pupils who are not native speakers of the standard language proficiency in writing in the standard language while respecting and helping to maintain their local nonstandard dialects. This policy, which is sometimes known as bidialectism, is normal in many countries, such as Switzerland, and is the only policy allowed by law in Norway. It is also the educational policy favoured by most sociolinguists involved in mother-tongue education.

bidialectism see **bidialectalism**

bilingualism The ability of an individual to speak two or more languages. In the usage of some writers, bilingualism refers only to individuals who have native command of more than one language. Other writers use the term to refer to any speaker who has a reasonable degree of competence in a language other than their mother tongue. Sociolinguists are agreed that bilingualism is so widespread in the world that there are probably more people in the world who are bilingual, at least in the second sense, than there are monolinguals. Many sociolinguists use the term 'bilingualism' to refer to individuals, even if they are trilingual, quadrilingual etc. and reserve the term **multilingualism** for nations or societies, even if only two languages are involved. See also **compound bilingualism** and **coordinate bilingualism**.

bioprogram hypothesis A hypothesis proposed by Derek Bickerton and discussed at length in his book *Roots of language*. Bickerton suggests that humans have a separate biological program for language and that the nature of this innate program is most open for study by linguists in the case of **creole** languages where communities of children have had to develop fully-fledged languages from limited and inadequate **pidgin** language sources. In other language communities, the bioprogram grammar will have been overridden by discourse needs and cultural developments. Creoles have linguistic characteristics in common and these similarities are due to the fact that their grammatical structures are derived directly from the bioprogram without any subsequent cultural overlay. This hypothesis might have implications for the study of the origins of human language.

Bislama An English-**lexifier** creole spoken in Vanuatu (formerly New Hebrides) and to a lesser extent in New Caledonia, South Pacific. It is also known as Bichelamar. Most users are non-native speakers who use the language as a **lingua franca**. It is historically related to and mutually intelligible to a fair degree with **Tok Pisin** and **Pijin**. The following is a version of the Lord's Prayer in Bislama:

> Papa bilong mifala,
> yu yu stap antap long heven,
> Mifala i wantem we nem bilong yu i tabu.
> Mifala i wantem we kingdom bilong yu i kam,
> Mo we olgeta man long wol oli wokem olgeta samting
>   we yu yu wantem,
> olsem olgeta long heven oli stap wokem.
> Mifala i askem yu bilong tedei yu givem kakai long
>   mifala,
> i stret bilong tedei nomo.
> Mifala i askem yu bilong yu fogivem mifala from ol
>   samting nogud bilong mifala,
> Olsem we mifala i stap fogivem ol man we oli stap
>   mekem i nogud long mifala.
> Mifala i askem yu bilong yu no tekem mifala i go long
>   sam samting we bambae oli traem mifala tumas,
> Mo bilong yu blokem Setan i no kam kasem mifala

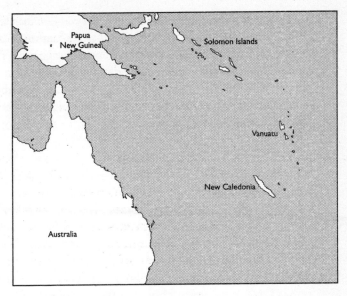

Vanuatu and New Caledonia

Black Vernacular English see **African American Vernacular English**

Bokmål /buːkmɔl/ One of the two officially recognised standard forms of Norwegian, the other being **Nynorsk**. When Norway gained independence from Denmark in the early nineteenth century, it was felt by many that Danish should be replaced as the official language by a standardised form of the closely related Scandinavian language Norwegian. There were two conflicting solutions to the problem of devising a Norwegian standard. One, promoted by Kud Knudsen (1812–95), was to make relatively minor changes to Danish in order to modify it in the direction of the speech of upper-class Norwegians in the capital Christiania (now Oslo). (For the other solution, see **Nynorsk**.) As a result of Norwegian governmental **language planning** policies, this form of Norwegian has gradually been modifed so that it is now less different from Nynorsk. Originally called Riksmål 'national language', it is now known as Bokmål 'book language'. The label Riksmål is still used to refer to an unofficial, more conservative (that is, less like Nynorsk) variety which is still favoured by some writers. The following is a text in Nynorsk and Bokmål which will permit a comparison:

Nynorsk	Bokmål
Begge dei to målformene våre er prega	Begge de to målformene våre er preget
av ein monaleg stor valfridom i	av en betydelig stor valgfridom i
rettskrivinga. Svært mange ord kan	rettskrivingen. Svært mange ord kan
både stavast og bøyast på ulike måtar utan	både staves og bøyes på forskellige måter uten
at det skal reknast for feil.	at det skal betraktes som feil.

'Both of the two forms of language are characterised by rather large freedom of choice in the orthography. Very many words can be both spelt and declined in different ways without that being considered a mistake.'

Bonin Islands Perhaps the least-known **anglophone** community in the world, these Japanese-owned islands (Japanese *Ogasawara-gunto*) are in the central Pacific Ocean, about 500 miles southeast of Japan. The population is about 2,000. The islands were discovered by the Spanish navigator Ruy Lopez de Villalobos in 1543. They were then claimed by the USA in 1823 and by Britain in 1825. The originally uninhabited islands were first settled in 1830 by five seamen – two Americans, one Englishman, one Dane and one Italian – together with ten Hawaiians, five men and five women. This founding population was later joined by whalers, shipwrecked sailors and drifters of many different origins. The islands were annexed by Japan in 1876. The English is mainly American in origin and has many similarities with New England varieties.

borrowing The process whereby bilingual speakers introduce words from one language into another language, these loan words eventually becoming accepted as an integral part of the second language. *Restaurant* was originally a French word, but is now an integral part of the English language and is known and used by all speakers of English whether or not they are bilingual in French. It is also pronounced by English speakers according to the rules of English and not French pronunciation. Loan words which are still in the process of being assimilated into another language may continue to be pronounced, as well as speakers are able, according to the rules of the original language, as with *coup d'état* in English. Grammatical constructions and speech sounds may also be borrowed from one language into another.

Bosnian see **Serbo-Croat**

Bourdieu, Pierre see **linguistic market**

British English The English of England, Scotland and Wales, not to be confused with **English English**.

bundles of isoglosses see **transition zone**

burnouts see **Belten High**

BVE see **African American Vernacular English**

C

Cajun /keidʒən/ Originally an abbreviated form of Acadian. Acadia is a term used to refer to the Maritime Provinces of Canada: New Brunswick, Nova Scotia and Prince Edward Island. In the 1750s, very many of the French-speaking settlers in these areas who had refused to swear allegiance to the Crown were expelled by the British, and many of them went to the French colony of Louisiana, now a state of the USA. Cajun French is the term used to refer to the variety of the French language still spoken in Louisiana by the descendants of these expellees. It retains a number of features of Canadian Maritime French, together with many **borrowings** from English. It is not to be confused with the French-based creole also spoken in Louisiana, mostly by African Americans.

Cashubian see **Kashubian**

Central American English Many areas of Central America are English-speaking rather than Spanish-speaking. The dialects are mostly of a Caribbean type. See **San Andrés and Providencia, Bay Islands, Miskito Coast, Corn Islands**.

Chambers, J. K. see **NORM**

change from above In terminology introduced by William Labov, linguistic changes which take place in a community above the level of conscious awareness, that is, when speakers have some awareness that they are making these changes. Very often, changes from above are made as a result of the influence of prestigious dialects with which the community is in contact, and the consequent **stigmatisation** of local dialect features. Changes from above therefore typically occur in the first instance in more closely monitored **styles**, and thus lead to **style stratification**. It is important to realise, however, that 'above' in this context does not refer to social class or status. It is not necessarily the case that such changes take place 'from above' socially. Change from above as a process is opposed by Labov to **change from below**.

change from below In terminology introduced by William Labov, linguistic changes which take place in a community below the level of conscious awareness, that is, when speakers are not consciously aware, unlike with **changes from above**, that such changes are taking place. Changes from below usually begin in one particular social class group, and thus lead to **class stratification**. While this particular social class group is very often not the highest class group in a society, it should be noted that change from below does not mean change 'from below' in any social sense.

Chatham Islands This island group is about 500 miles east of New Zealand. The inhabited islands are Chatham Island and Pitt Island, which is about 12 miles to the southeast. The indigenous population were the Polynesian Moriori, who were conquered and exterminated by the New Zealand Maori after 1835. The islands were annexed by New Zealand in 1842. The current population of about 750 is mainly white with some people of Maori or mixed Maori and Moriori origin. The English dialect is similar to that of New Zealand.

Chicano From Spanish *mejicano* 'Mexican', a term used in the USA (particularly in the southwest) to refer to people living in the country, including American citizens, who are of Mexican origin. The term is then extended in sociolinguistics to refer to the English and/or Spanish that Chicanos speak. The feminine form is 'Chicana'.

class stratification A term from **secular linguistics** which refers to the relationship between language and social class, whereby certain variants of a **linguistic variable** are used most often by higher-class speakers, and other variants most frequently by lower-class speakers. Speakers from intermediate classes will use these variants with intermediate frequency, or else will use intermediate variants. As a result of **t-glottaling**, many British communities have class stratification of the variable (t) – the pronunciation of /t/ in *better*, *bet* etc. – with the variant [t] being used more frequently by higher-class speakers and the variant [ʔ] being used more frequently by lower-class speakers.

classical language A language which has the characteristics of **autonomy** and **standardisation** but which does not have the characteristic of **vitality**, that is, although it used to have native speakers, it no longer does so. Classical European languages include Latin and Ancient Greek. The ancient Indian language Sanskrit, an ancestor of modern North Indian languages such as Hindi and Bengali, is another example of a classical language, as is Classical Arabic. Classical languages generally survive because they are written languages which are known non-natively as a result of being used for purposes of religion or scholarship. Latin has been associated with Catholicism, Sanskrit with Hinduism, and Classical Arabic with Islam.

cline A term associated with the work of Michael Halliday and used in **functional sociolinguistics** to apply to a continuum of infinite gradation in language.

Clonard see **Belfast**

Cockney A term used to refer to people, usually of working-class origin, from the East End of London, and, by extension, to the accent and dialect of English spoken by such people. The accent is characterised by **l-vocalisation**, **t-glottaling** and **th-fronting**.

Cocoliche /kokolitʃe/ A linguistic variety which is a mixture of Spanish and Italian, spoken by some people of Italian origin in Argentina.

code-mixing The process whereby speakers indulge in **code-switching** between languages of such rapidity and density, even within sentences and phrases, that it is not really possible to say at any given time which language they are speaking. There are many reports from countries such as Malta, Nigeria and Hong Kong of educated elites indulging in code-mixing, using a mixture of English and the local language. Sociolinguistic explanations for this behaviour normally concentrate on the possibility, through using code-mixing as a strategy, of projecting two identities at once, for example that of a modern, sophisticated, educated person *and* that of a loyal, local patriot (see **act of identity**).

code-switching The process whereby bilingual or bidialectal speakers switch back and forth between one language or dialect and another within the same conversation. This linguistic behaviour is very common in multilingual situations. Sociolinguistic research in this area has concentrated on trying to establish what factors in the social and linguistic context influence switching: it may be that one language is typically associated with one set of **domains**, and the other language with another. Research has also focused on what are the grammatical rules for where switching can and cannot take place, and the extent to which it is possible to distinguish between code-switching and **borrowing**.

codification The process whereby a **variety** of a **language**, often as part of a **standardisation** process, acquires a publicly recognised and fixed form in which norms are laid down for 'correct' usage as far as grammar, vocabulary, spelling and perhaps pronunciation are concerned. This codification can take place over time without involvement of official bodies, as happened with **Standard English,** or it can take place quite rapidly, as a result of conscious decisions by governmental or other official planning agencies, as happened with Swahili in Tanzania. The results of codification are usually enshrined in dictionaries and grammar books, as well as, sometimes, in government publications.

coherence A term used in **discourse analysis** and other related areas to refer to semantic well-connectedness between different parts of a text.

cohesion A term used in **discourse analysis** and other related areas to refer to grammatical well-connectedness between different parts of a text.

colloquial A term used to apply to varieties and forms that are towards the very informal end of the formal-informal stylistic continuum. See **style.**

communicative competence A term introduced by the American anthropological linguist Dell Hymes by analogy with Chomsky's term **competence** – the native speaker's (unconscious) linguistic knowledge of the structure of his or her language. Hymes points out that knowing the grammar, phonology and lexicon of a language is not enough. All native speakers of a language also have to know how to *use* that language appropriately in the society in which they live. They have to know when to speak and when not to, which greeting formula to use when, which style to use in which situation, and so on. Non-native speakers also have to acquire communicative as well as linguistic competence when learning a foreign language, if they are to be able to use that language effectively and appropriately and to participate in **cross-cultural communication**. The **ethnography of speaking** involves the study of what is necessary to be communicatively competent in different communities.

community of practice A sociological concept referring to a group of people who associate with one another in some joint activity and who share a set of social practices. The term normally refers to groups rather smaller than those indicated by the term **speech community**. The emphasis is on the subjective nature of people's perceptions of this community and of the boundaries between it and other communities, and on the way in which this community is negotiated, constructed and modified by its members in interaction with each other. In sociolinguistics, the best known work employing this notion is that of Penelope Eckert. See **Belten High**.

complication The process associated with **decreolisation** and **depidginisation** in which the **simplification** which has taken place during **pidginisation** is 'repaired' as a result of **language contact** between the **creole** or **pidgin** and the **source language**. Complication thus takes the form of the reintroduction of irregularities etc. that are present in the source language but absent in the creole or pidgin.

compound bilingualism A term associated with the work of Uriel Weinreich. A form of individual bilingualism in which speakers supposedly have one set of concepts which are related to two different sets of words in two different languages. See also **coordinate bilingualism**.

constraints In **variation theory**, linguistic and social factors which have been shown to influence linguistic variation.

For instance, the simplification of consonant clusters in English, as in *old > ol'*, *left > lef'*, *west > wes'*, is variable: most speakers sometimes simplify these clusters and sometimes do not. This variation, however, is not random (although one can never predict in any given instance whether it will occur or not). The probability that a consonant cluster will be simplified depends on a number of factors which influence or constrain this variability. There are phonological constraints, with simplification being more frequent before consonants, as in *west side*, than before vowels, as in *west end*; grammatical constraints, with simplification being less frequent where grammatical endings are involved, as in *left them*, than where they are not, as in *left side*; and *stylistic* constraints, with simplification being more frequent in informal than in formal situations.

consultant see **informant**

convergence see **accommodation**

conversation analysis An area of sociolinguistics with links to **ethnomethodology** which analyses the structure and norms of conversation in **face-to-face interaction**. Conversation analysts look at aspects of conversation such as the relationship between questions and answers, or summonses and responses. They are also concerned with rules for conversational discourse, such as those involving **turn-taking**; with conversational devices such as **discourse markers**; and with norms for participating in conversation, such as the rules for interruption, for changing topic, for overlapping between one speaker and another, for remaining silent, for closing a conversation, and so on. In so far as norms for conversational interaction may vary from society to society, conversation analysis may also have links with **cross-cultural communication** and the **ethnography of speaking**. By some writers it is opposed to discourse analysis.

conversational implicature A term introduced by the British philosopher Paul Grice. Something which is deduced or inferred, by employing the **cooperative principle**, from what someone has said, even though they have not actually said it. Consider the following conversation:

A: Are you going on holiday this year?
B: I haven't got any money.

B has not actually answered A's question as such, but a clear answer is implied, given that both parties share the assumption that holidays cost money.

conversational maxims The four sub-principles which underly Grice's **cooperative principle**: 'Be as informative as necessary but no more so'; 'Be relevant'; 'Be clear' and 'Be genuine'.

cooperative principle The principle developed by the philosopher Paul Grice that participants in a conversation normally cooperate with each other in order to produce a successful conversation, and that it is therefore legitimate for any participant to assume that any other participant is being cooperative. For example, it is legitimate to assume that a response which follows a question is intended as an answer. See also **conversational maxims**, **conversational implicature**.

coordinate bilingualism A term associated with the work of Uriel Weinreich. A form of individual bilingualism in which speakers supposedly have two different sets of concepts which are related to two different sets of words in two different languages. See also **compound bilingualism**.

Copper Island Aleut A fascinating and unusual language, now probably extinct or almost so, which is the product of **language intertwining**. It is the result of an unusually intimate mixture of Russian and Aleut. (Aleut is a member of the Eskimo-Aleut language family which is spoken by perhaps 2,000 people on the Aleutian islands of the northern Pacific Ocean between Alaska and Siberia, which are divided administratively between the USA and Russia.) In this mixture, the vocabulary and noun-phrase morphology is mostly of Aleutian origin, but the verbal morphology and the syntax is mainly Russian.

copula absence see **copula deletion**

copula deletion A feature of a number of **dialects** of English, notably **African American Vernacular English**. In these dialects, forms of the copula (the verb *to be*) are variably absent in certain grammatical and phonological contexts. Thus it is grammatical in these dialects to say *He nice* or *We coming* or *She a teacher*, but not, for example, **I know who you*. Many **creole** languages also lack the copula in these positions, as do many non-creole languages such as Russian and Hungarian, but since this is not a variable feature of these languages, it is better to refer in these cases to 'copula absence' rather than 'copula deletion'.

Corn Islands The Corn Islands of Nicaragua, Great and Little Corn Island, which are about fifty miles offshore from the **Miskito Coast** town of Bluefields, are inhabited by people, mostly of African origin, who are native speakers of a Caribbean type of **Central American English**.

corpus planning An aspect of **language planning** and **codification** in which decisions are taken about the linguistic characteristics of the variety of language in question. Typical corpus planning issues involve questions concerning which pronunciation to use of those available; which syntactic structures and morphological forms are to be permitted; which of a number of regionally based words of identical meaning is to be favoured; and what is to be done about expansion of the vocabulary, if this is thought to be necessary. Corpus planning is usually contrasted with **status planning**. See also **language development**.

correctness In **speech communities** which have been subject to considerable focusing (see **focused**), native speakers tend to have notions about which linguistic forms are correct and which are not. Linguists agree that the language of non-native speakers can be labelled 'incorrect' if it contains constructions or usages that would never be employed by native speakers, such as *I am knowing him since many years*. They do not agree, however, that judgements about correctness can legitimately be made about forms used by native speakers. They point out that when such judgements are made about forms in widespread use, such as *I done it*, they are essentially social judgements which have to do with the distribution of power, wealth and prestige in a community. See also **prescriptive**, **language myths**, **folk linguistics**.

correlational sociolinguistics A term applied by some writers to the work of linguists like William Labov who in their research have correlated **linguistic variables** with social parameters such as sex, age and social class. The term, however, is never used by the practitioners of this type of work, and should be avoided in favour of other terms such as **secular linguistics**, since it implies that the correlation is central and an end in itself rather than what it actually is, namely a means to an end – a methodology for studying phenomena such as linguistic change.

covert prestige A term introduced by William Labov in his 1966 book *The social stratification of English in New York City* to refer to the favourable connotations that nonstandard or apparently low-status or 'incorrect' forms have for many speakers. Standard words, pronunciations and grammatical forms have overt prestige in that they are publicly acknowledged as 'correct' and as bestowing high social status on their users. We have to assume, however, that nonstandard and apparently low-status forms do also have a kind of less publicly acknowledged or hidden prestige which leads their users to continue to use them. The covert prestige associated with such linguistic forms bestows status on their users as being members of their local community and as having desirable qualities such as friendliness and loyalty. Covert prestige emerges in **under-reporting** in **self report tests** when speakers claim to use linguistic features which have lower social status than those which they actually use.

creole A language which has undergone considerable **pidginisation** but where the **reduction** associated with pidginisation has been repaired by a process of **expansion** or creolisation, as a result of its having acquired a community of native speakers and of being employed for an increasingly wide range of purposes. Creoles which have not undergone any **decreolisation** are not normally intelligible to speakers of the original **source language**. Some of the better-known creoles include English-based creoles like the Sranan of Surinam, French-based creoles such as Haitian Creole, and Portuguese-based creoles such as that of the Cape Verde Islands, but by no means all of them are based on European languages. It is a common but undesirable practice to refer to any language which has undergone **admixture** as a creole. See also **bioprogram hypothesis.**

creolisation see **creole**

creoloid A language which, as a result of **language contact,** has experienced **simplification** and **admixture,** but has not undergone the **reduction** associated with full pidginisation (nor, therefore, the **expansion** associated with creolisation). Such a language will resemble in its linguistic characteristics a **creole** which has undergone **decreolisation,** but will be different in its history: a creoloid remains at all times intelligible to speakers of its **source language** if this remains separate from the creoloid; and it maintains throughout its development a community of native speakers. A good example of a creoloid is the South African language Afrikaans, which is historically a form of Dutch which has undergone a certain amount of simplification and admixture in a multilingual contact situation. Some writers have argued that English is in origin a creoloid: a simplified, mixed form of Old English that arose in the Old English-Norman French-Old Norse contact situation.

critical discourse analysis A form of discourse analysis which seeks to establish the underlying assumptions and hidden (often political) biases in a particular text.

critical linguistics The techniques of linguistic analysis employed by practitioners of **critical discourse analysis.**

critical period hypothesis The hypothesis that human beings are genetically programmed to learn perfectly languages to which they have sufficient exposure up to a certain age, but that then after this age-threshold has been passed, this ability shuts down, with the result that adolescents and adults are generally not good language learners. There is no general agreement as to the location of this threshold, and indeed there is probably a lot of variation from one person to another, but it is probably somewhere between eight and fourteen. This hypothesis is important in the development of theories about the origins of **pidgin** and **creole** languages. This is because **pidginisation** can be attributed to the learning of languages by speakers who have passed beyond the critical period.

critical threshold see **critical period hypothesis**

Croatian see **Serbo-Croat**

cross-cultural communication Communication between speakers from different cultural backgrounds, which can often be difficult because of different assumptions about when, why and how language is to be used. As demonstrated by the **ethnography of speaking**, different communities have different norms for how language is to be employed. Cross-cultural communication does not necessarily imply that different languages are involved. Speakers of Australian English whose families are of Greek origin, for example, have been shown to have different ideas about the use of irony than speakers of the same language who are of British Isles origin.

Csángó There is a very large Hungarian-speaking minority in Romanian Transylvania. It is not widely known, however, that there is also another Hungarian or 'Hungarian' speaking minority in Moldavia in eastern Romania. These are the Csángos, who are a mostly ignored linguistic minority rapidly going through a process of language shift to Romanian and who are distinguished from other Romanians by their poverty, isolation and Catholicism. Romanian governments have sometimes denied their Hungarianness. Now the Csángos are faced with the reverse kind of **Ausbau** problem. Since 1989, Hungarian official bodies have been concerned to 'save the Csángos'. They assume that Csángos are Hungarian-speakers and that young people will benefit from being offered education in Hungary or Transylvania. There is, however, too much **Abstand** for this to work easily. Csángo is also widely regarded in Hungary as 'corrupt Hungarian', which gives the Csángos an additional reason to switch to Romanian.

curvilinear principle The principle, developed by William Labov, that linguistic **change from below** normally originates in a social group which is neither at the bottom nor the top of the social hierarchy, but somewhere in the middle. If a **linguistic variable** which is involved in such a change is plotted quantitatively on a graph against social class, it will thus produce a curvilinear pattern.

D

dachlos see **roofless dialects**

dead language A dead language is one which no longer has any native speakers. See **language death**.

debt incurred, principle of see **linguistic gratuity**

decreolisation A situation which arises when a **creole** language remains or comes back into contact with its original **source language**, and is influenced linguistically by the source language if, as is often the case, the source language has higher prestige. Speakers of the creole will accommodate (see **accommodation**) to the source language, and the creole will become more like the source language. The original **pidginisation**, which led to the development of the pidgin precursor of the creole, involved the processes of **reduction, simplification** and **admixture**. The reduction will already have been 'repaired' by the process of **expansion** during creolisation. Decreolisation thus consists linguistically of two processes, one which counteracts the simplification, namely **complication**, and another which removes the admixture, namely **purification**. Decreolisation often leads to the development of a **post-creole continuum**.

deficit hypothesis see **verbal deprivation**

dense see **network strength**

depidginisation The linguistic processes of **complication, purification** (see **decreolisation**) and **expansion**, by which a **pidgin** or pidginised (see **pidginisation**) variety of language comes to resemble or become identical with the **source language** from which it was originally derived. This may occur if speakers of the pidgin or pidginised variety have extensive contacts with speakers of the source language.

determination see **language determination and status planning**

development see **language development**

diachronic, diachronically literally 'through time', hence 'historical', the opposite of synchronic. Diachronic linguistics is thus linguistics which is historical and which looks at linguistic change through time.

dialect A **variety** of language which differs grammatically, phonologically and lexically from other varieties, and which is associated with a particular geographical area and/or with a particular social class or status group (see also **sociolect**). Varieties which differ from one another only in pronunciation are known as **accents**. Varieties which are associated only with particular social situations are known as **styles**. Neither of these should be confused with dialect. The term is often used to refer only to **nonstandard dialects** or to **traditional dialects**. Strictly speaking, however, standard varieties such as **Standard English** are just as much dialects as any other dialect. A **language** is typically composed of a number of dialects.

dialect area see **transition zone**

dialect atlas see **linguistic atlas**

dialect contact Contact between linguistic **varieties** which results from communication between speakers of different but **mutually intelligible** dialects, often involving **accommodation**. Such communication is of course very common indeed, but, from the point of view of sociolinguistics, such contacts are particularly interesting where they occur on a large scale, such as at dialect boundaries (see **isogloss**) or as a result of urbanisation or colonisation. In these cases, phenomena such as **dialect mixture** and **hyperadaptation** may occur.

dialect continuum (plural: **continua**) A very common situation in which geographically neighbouring dialects, particularly **traditional** rural **dialects**, differ from one another minimally but in which the further one travels from any starting point the more different dialects become. All dialects will be intelligible to speakers of neighbouring dialects, but the greater the distance between locations where dialects are spoken, the more difficult comprehension will be. If the geographical area in question is large enough, dialects which are linked to one another by a chain of mutual intelligibility of intervening dialects may nevertheless themselves not be mutually intelligible. The Low German dialects of Schleswig-Holstein, northern Germany, are part of the same dialect continuum as the Swiss German dialects of central Switzerland, and are linked to them by a chain of mutual intelligibility – there is nowhere on the continuum where speakers cannot understand the dialects of neighbouring villages – but they are not mutually intelligible (see **West Germanic dialect continuum**). Dialect continua can also be social, with **sociolects** changing gradually as one moves up or down the social scale (see **Jamaican Creole**). See also **acrolect, basilect, mesolect, North Slavic dialect continuum, South Slavic dialect continuum, West Romance dialect continuum.**

dialect mixture A consequence of large-scale, long-term **dialect contact** in which **face-to-face interaction** between speakers of different dialects, stemming from developments such as emigration or urbanisation, leads to **accommodation** between these speakers and thus the mixing of different **dialect** forms. The end result of the mixture may ultimately be the formation of a new dialect, such as Australian English, with speakers selecting a combination of forms from different dialects which are present in the mixture for retention, and discarding others. The new dialect will typically have the linguistic characteristics of a **koiné**.

dialectology The academic study of dialects, often associated especially with the phonological, morphological and lexical study of rural **traditional dialects**, which were the original concern of this discipline, and the spatial or geographical distribution of traditional dialect forms (see **traditional dialectology**). In more recent years, however, dialectologists have also been concerned with syntactic features, with **urban dialectology**, with social dialectology, and with the social distribution of linguistic forms (see **sociolects**).

dialectometry A form of spatial **dialectology**, which has links with **geolinguistics** (1) and with **traditional dialectology**. Dialectometry is associated particularly with the work of Jean Séguy, and involves the study of (for the most part) **traditional dialects** using quantitative and computerised methodology for the location and weighting of **isoglosses**.

dialect-switching see **divergent dialect community**

diasystem A notion developed by Uriel Weinreich in which a higher-level (usually phonological) system incorporates two or more dialect systems and shows the similarities and differences between them and in particular the systematic nature of correspondences between them. For example, a diasystem portraying the short vowel systems of northern and southern English might look like this:

$$\text{North, South } /\!/ i \approx e \approx æ \frac{N \quad u}{S \; u \sim \Lambda} \approx o /\!/$$

This demonstrates that northern English dialects have the same vowel in the lexical sets of *but* and *put* and thus have one fewer vowel than southern English dialects.

diatopic Literally 'through space', hence 'spatial'. Diatopic variation in language is thus the same as geographical variation.

diffuse According to a typology of language varieties developed by the British sociolinguist Robert B. LePage, a characteristic of certain language communities, and thus language varieties. Some communities are relatively more diffuse, while others are relatively more **focused**. Any speech act performed by an individual constitutes an **act of identity**. If a wide range of identities is available for enactment in a **speech community**, that community can be regarded as diffuse. Diffuse linguistic communities tend to be those where little **standardisation** or **codification** have taken place, where there is relatively little agreement about norms of usage, where speakers show little concern for marking off their language variety from other varieties, and where they may accord relatively little importance even to what their language is called.

diffusion (1) The process whereby words, pronunciations or grammatical forms spread or diffuse from one variety to another. To do this, forms must spread from one speaker to another via **face-to-face interaction** in situations of **dialect contact**, in which speakers of different dialects may **accommodate** to each other and, if interaction is frequent enough, permanently acquire features from other dialects. Diffusion may be geographical, in which forms spread from one area (and thus geographical dialect) to another, or social, in which forms spread from one social group (and thus **sociolect**) to another. 'Diffusion' can also be used of the geographical spread of a **language**, often at the expense of another through **language shift**, or as a result of **language planning**. (2) The carrying out of **speech acts** and other processes whereby speech communities become **diffuse**, in the sense of LePage.

diglossia (1) A term associated with the American linguist Charles A. Ferguson which describes sociolinguistic situations such as those that obtain in Arabic-speaking countries and in German-speaking Switzerland. In such a diglossic community, the prestigious standard or 'High' (or H) **variety**, which is linguistically related to but significantly different from the **vernacular** or 'Low' (or L) **varieties**, has no native speakers. All members of the speech community are native speakers of one of the L varieties, such as Colloquial Arabic and Swiss German, and learn the H variety, such as Classical Arabic and Standard German, at school. H varieties are typically used in writing and in high-status spoken **domains** where preparation of what is to be said or read is possible. L varieties are used in all other contexts. (2) Ferguson's original term was later extended by the American sociolinguist Joshua Fishman to include sociolinguistic situations other than those where the H and L varieties are varieties of the same language, such as Arabic or German. In Fishman's usage, even multilingual countries such as Nigeria, where English functions as a nationwide prestige language which is learnt in school and local languages such as Hausa and Yoruba are spoken natively, are described as being diglossic. In these cases, languages such as English are described as H varieties, and languages such as Yoruba as L.

diminutive The opposite of **augmentative**. A form, usually of a noun, with the added meaning of 'little'. In European languages this is usually signalled by a suffix, as in English *notelet* from *note*, Greek *pedhaki* 'small child' from *pedhi* 'child', or French *fillette* 'small girl' from *fille*. There is frequently an associated meaning of endearment. See also **hypocoristic**.

discourse analysis A branch of linguistics which deals with linguistic units at levels above the sentence, that is texts and conversations. Those branches of discourse analysis which come under the heading of sociolinguistics presuppose that language is being used in social interaction and thus deal with conversation. Other non-sociolinguistic branches of discourse analysis are often known as text linguistics. Discourse analysis is opposed by some writers to **conversation analysis**.

discourse marker Units recognised by linguists working in **conversation analysis** and **discourse analysis**. Discourse markers are words, phrases or sounds which have no real lexical meaning but have instead an important function in marking conversational structure, in signalling the conversational intentions of speakers and in securing cooperation and responses from listeners. Discourse markers in English include *well*, *oh*, *actually*, *OK*, *now*, and so on.

discreteness A term meaning 'separateness' often used in sociolinguistics to contrast with 'continuity' as, for example, in **dialect continuum**.

distance see **Abstand language**

divergence see **accommodation**

divergence controversy A controversy between certain American linguists about the relationship between **African Amerian Vernacular English** and other varieties of American English. It is generally agreed amongst American linguists that **AAVE** has converged on White varieties of English over the centuries, that is, it is now more similar to White dialects than it used to be, and may even be a decreolised **creole**. However, data obtained by sociolinguists from the 1980s has been interpreted by some as indicating that it is once again diverging from White varieties, perhaps as a result of the increasing ghettoisation and residential separation of White and Black Americans. Other linguists disagree with this analysis, and dispute the data and/or its interpretation.

divergent dialect community A **speech community** in which the **vernacular variety** is linguistically very different from the prestige or standard variety. In such communities, there may exist a very long social **dialect continuum**, such as a **post-creole continuum**. Alternatively, if no such continuum exists, the clear linguistic separation of vernacular and standard may lead to **code-switching** or dialect-switching between the varieties. Diglossic communities (see **diglossia** [1]) are a special case of divergent communities. Sociolinguists encounter different methodological problems in divergent dialect communities than in other communities, particularly in the setting up of **linguistic variables**. Within the English-speaking world, divergent dialect communities are to be found in the Caribbean and in Northern Britain and northern Ireland. Communities in North America and southern England (except for speakers of **traditional dialects**) typically speak dialects which are linguistically much more similar to **Standard English**.

Djuka see **Ndjuka**

domain A concept employed particularly in studies of **code-switching** in multilingual contexts and in the study of other situations where different **languages**, **dialects** or **styles** are used in different **social contexts**. A domain is a combination of factors which are believed to influence choice of code (language, dialect or style) by speakers. Such factors might include participants (in a conversation), topic and location. For example, the domestic domain, which would probably produce an informal style of speech, might involve the home location, family participants and a day-to-day topic.

domestic domain see **domain**

double negative see **multiple negation**

dual-source see **Pitkern, Russenorsk**

E

Ebonics A journalistic term, generally avoided by linguists, for **African American Vernacular English.** The term gained some notoriety during the controversy surrounding the educational proposals made by the school board of **Oakland,** California.

Eckert, Penelope see **Belten High, community of practice**

educational linguistics The application of the findings of linguistics, particularly **sociolinguistics,** to the solution of educational problems, especially those associated with mother-tongue education such as the role of **nonstandard dialect** in the classroom.

EFL see **English as a foreign language**

elaborated code A concept developed by the British sociologist Basil Bernstein in connection with his work on language use, social class and socialisation. Elaborated code, originally called 'public language', is a form of language use which, according to Bernstein, is characterised by a high degree of explicitness, and is therefore suitable for public use in situations where participants do not have a large fund of shared knowledge or assumptions in common. Elaborated code is thought of as lying at the opposite end of a continuum of types of language use from **restricted code**. Bernstein argued that some working-class children in Britain were disadvantaged in the education system because they were unable to use elaborated code. Bernstein's theory aroused considerable hostility on the part of linguists in its initial formulation as it discussed – irrelevantly, as it now seems – grammatical features, such as pronouns and relative clauses, and was interpreted by some educationists as having some link to **Standard English**. Elaborated code in fact has no connection with any **dialect**, but is rather concerned, as part of a theory of language use and social structure, with the content of what speakers say.

embedding problem One of a number of problems pointed to by the American sociolinguist William Labov in connection with the study of linguistic change within the field of **secular linguistics**. It is the problem, in the study of linguistic changes as they are actually taking place, of locating and analysing both the linguistic and social settings in which the changes are occurring. In the study of sound change, the linguist has to look not only at structural pressures in the sound system, as was the practice in pre-Labovian historical linguistics, but also – and simultaneously – at the social background against which the change is taking place. The change has to be situated in a matrix of both linguistic and social factors.

endogenous minority language A language spoken by a **linguistic minority** in a country and which is not the majority language in any other country, such as Basque, which is a minority language in Spain and France, and is nowhere a majority language.

English as a foreign language (EFL) Countries in which English is a foreign language are those such as Germany, Japan or Morocco where English is not spoken as a native language, and where it does not have any important or official role within the country i.e. it is normally learnt and used to permit communication with English **native speakers** and with other non-native speakers from outside the country.

English as a second language (ESL) Countries in which English is a second language are those such as Pakistan, Nigeria or Fiji where English is not spoken as a native language but where it has an important or official role as a means of communication within the country in the education system and/or the media and/or the government.

English English The English of England (as opposed to Australia, Canada and so on). Not to be confused with **British English**. Also less happily known as 'Anglo-English'.

Eskilstuna The town in central Sweden where the first large-scale, quantitative sociolinguistic study of a dialect of Swedish was undertaken by Bengt Nordberg and associates, starting in the 1960s.

ESL see **English as a second language**

ethnic group An important concept both in **language planning** studies and in certain types of **secular linguistics**. An ethnic group is a sociocultural group or 'race' of people who feel themselves to be members of a social entity which is distinct from other social groups, and with a culture that is distinct from that of other groups. As defined by the American sociolinguist Joshua Fishman, an ethnic group is smaller and more locality-bound than a **nationality**, but this distinction is not maintained by all writers. There is in any case a continuum of size and locality-boundedness along which groups of people can be ranged. Thus it is not unusual for groups as different in size – and relative size within their own nation (see **nationism**) – as African Americans, Scandinavian Sami, Icelanders and Ukrainians to be referred to as constituting ethnic groups.

ethnography of communication A term identical in reference to **ethnography of speaking**, except that nonverbal communication is also included. For example, proxemics – the study of factors such as how physically close to each other speakers may be, in different cultures, when communicating with one another – could be discussed under this heading.

ethnography of speaking A branch of **sociolinguistics** or **anthropological linguistics** particularly associated with the American scholar Dell Hymes. The ethnography of speaking studies the norms and rules for using language in social situations in different cultures and is thus clearly important for **cross-cultural communication**. The concept of **communicative competence** is a central one in the ethnography of speaking. Crucial topics include the study of who is allowed to speak to who – and when; what types of language are to be used in different contexts; how to do things with language, such as make requests or tell jokes; how much **indirectness** it is normal to employ; how often it is usual to speak, and how much one should say; how long it is permitted to remain silent; and the use of formulaic language such as expressions used for greeting, leave-taking and thanking.

ethnolect A **variety** of language associated with a particular ethnic group, such as **Angloromany**.

ethnolinguistic vitality A concept developed by Howard Giles and used to refer to the amount of dynamism present in a particular linguistic community. The term is normally used with reference to **linguistic minorities** and the likelihood of their languages surviving or becoming subject to **language shift** and **language death**. See also **vitality**.

ethnomethodology A branch of sociology which has links with certain sorts of **sociolinguistics** such as **conversation analysis** because of its use of recorded conversational material as data. Most ethnomethodologists, however, are generally not interested in the language of conversation as such but rather in the content of what is said. They study not language or speech, but **talk**. In particular, they are interested in what is *not* said. They focus on the shared common-sense knowledge speakers have of their society which they can leave unstated in conversation because it is taken for granted by all participants.

expansion Part of the process of creolisation in which the **reduction** which has occurred during **pidginisation** is repaired, as the **creole** acquires native speakers and/or is used in a wider range of functions. Expansion involves an increase in the vocabulary of the language, as well as the development of an often much wider range of grammatical and stylistic devices. Sometimes this development may take place with the help of external stimuli, such as when words are borrowed from other languages. Other developments may be language-internal, such as when new words are coined, by compounding or some other means, from words already available in the language. As far as grammatical expansion is concerned, it is the development of grammatical categories and devices without external stimuli that is the focus of the **bioprogram hypothesis**, the interest centring on the possibility that new features are generated directly from the innate human language faculty itself.

exogenous minority language A language which is spoken by a **linguistic minority** in a country but is the majority language in some other country, such as Slovenian, which is a minority language in Austria and Italy, but the majority language in Slovenia.

eye dialect A term used to refer to the representation of **nonstandard dialects** in writing, particularly with reference to spellings such as <wot> for *what* where the spelling does not actually indicate a pronunciation different from that represented by the standard orthography, and where it rather has the role of simply indicating that the speaker is using a nonstandard dialect or low prestige accent. For example, writing <o> instead of <a> in *what* actually tells us nothing about the vowel the speaker is supposed to be using and is probably rather a way of indicating that the speaker is using a **glottal stop** at the end of the word rather than [t].

F

face In a conversation, a speaker's face consists of the positive impression of themselves that they wish to make on the other participants. If such an impression is not successfully conveyed or is not accepted by the other participants, loss of face will result. Face, however, is not the sole responsibility of the individual concerned. In many forms of **face-to-face interaction**, all participants will be concerned to maintain not only their own face but also that of the others. See also **negative politeness** and **positive politeness**.

face-to-face interaction Conversation or communication between two or more people which is interactive (e.g. it is not a monologue), and in which the participants are physically present (e.g. they are not talking on the telephone). Studies of face-to-face interaction are important in the **social psychology of language**; **conversation analysis**; studies of **positive politeness** and **negative politeness**; and in studies of **accommodation** and **diffusion**.

familiar forms see **T and V pronouns**

Fanagaló Also Fanakalo. A pidgin language dating from the 1800s whose main **lexifier** is Zulu but which also has about twenty-five per cent of its vocabulary derived from English, with some Afrikaans also. It is mainly spoken in South Africa, particularly in mining areas, but is also used in Namibia, Zambia and Zimbabwe.

Ferguson, Charles see **diglossia**

fine stratification In Labovian **secular linguistics**, **linguistic variables** are employed to investigate **social stratification** and **style stratification**. This stratification can take the form of fine stratification or **sharp stratification**. In fine stratification, correlations between social factors and scores for linguistic variables show that there is a continuum between one social group or style and another, rather than a series of sharp breaks in linguistic behaviour.

first language A language (or languages) which a speaker learns first, from infancy, as their native language or mother-tongue. Compare **primary language**.

Fishman, Joshua see **diglossia, ethnic group, nationality, nationism**

focal area A concept from **traditional dialectology** and more recent work in **dialectometry**, **geolinguistics** (1), and spatial **dialectology**. Traditional dialectologists discovered early on in the history of the discipline that **isoglosses** for individual words and pronunciations rarely coincided with each other. One reaction to that finding was to suggest that there was no such thing as a dialect totally distinct from other dialects. This is in most cases strictly-speaking correct (see **dialect continuum**), but it is not simply the case that isoglosses are randomly distributed. Dialect features show different types of geographical patterning. Some geographical areas are crossed by no or relatively few isoglosses. These are central focal areas or kernel areas from which linguistic innovations have spread to surrounding areas. Such focal areas are in turn surrounded by **transition zones** which separate them from other focal areas. Focal areas often centre on influential urban areas or on means of communication such as roads or rivers.

focused According to a typology of language varieties developed by the British sociolinguist Robert B. LePage, some language communities and thus language varieties are relatively more **diffuse**, while others are relatively more focused. Any speech act performed by an individual constitutes an **act of identity**. If only a narrow range of identities is available for enactment in a **speech community**, that community can be regarded as focused. Focused linguistic communities tend to be those where considerable **standardisation** and **codification** have taken place, where there is a high degree of agreement about norms of usage, where speakers tend to show concern for 'purity' and marking their language variety off from other varieties, and where everyone agrees about what the language is called. European language communities tend to be heavily focused. LePage points out that notions such as **admixture, code-mixing, code-switching, semilingualism** and **multilingualism** depend on a focused-language-centred point of view of the separate status of language varieties.

focusing The process whereby language varieties become **focused**.

folk etymology A process whereby speakers alter the form of a word, usually a word of foreign or learned origin, to make it resemble something which makes more sense to them in terms of their own language variety, such as English *crayfish* from French *écrevisse*, and American English *woodchuck* from Algonquian *otchek*. The effect of this process is to increase the amount of apparent **semantic transparency**.

folk linguistics This term can refer to what members of a speech community know, or believe they know, about their language, and about language in general, as well as to the study of these beliefs by linguists.

foreigner talk A way of talking to foreigners, or, better, non-native speakers, who are not able – or who are thought not to be able – to understand normal fluent speech in a particular language. This term is particularly useful for describing aspects of the language used to foreigners which are institutionalised, i.e. there are norms in the language community, which are learned by people growing up in that community, for how one should speak to non-native speakers. These norms may include grammatical **simplification** such as *Me go, you stay* and the use of certain words (such as English *savvy?*) which may well not be known to foreigners at all. Foreigner talk is thought by many to be of interest in the formation of **pidgins**.

forensic sociolinguistics The use of sociolinguistic knowledge and techniques in the investigation of crime, and in the prosecution and defence of people accused of crimes. Sociolinguists have been employed, for instance, to demonstrate that a defendant could not have made a telephone call recorded by police because his dialect did not tally with that on the recording; and to decode recordings of communication between criminals speaking in an **antilanguage** such as **Pig Latin**.

formal forms see **T and V pronouns**

fossilisation A term used to describe a situation where a non-native learner of a language reaches a particular stage of proficiency and then stops, such that **interlanguage** features become permanent in their usage. In sociolinguistics, fossilisation is of particular interest for the study of the development of **pidgin** languages.

francophone French-speaking

Franco-Provençal A group of dialects from the **West Romance dialect continuum** which are or were spoken in all of western Switzerland except for the Jura mountain area, the neighbouring area of eastern central France including the regions around Lyons and Grenoble, and in the Val d'Aosta in Italy. It is today sometimes considered to be a dialect of French, and as a consequence the Val d'Aosta has been designated an officially French-Italian bilingual area. However, the linguistic differences from French are considerable, with the linguistic characteristics of the dialects being intermediate between those of French and **Occitan**. Although the dialects in Italy are thriving, the Swiss dialects are now extinct except in some small areas in the cantons of Fribourg and Valais. Franco-Provençal has never really been a language as such in that it never achieved true **autonomy**, although it was used in writing for some purposes under the Kingdom of Savoy. To illustrate the degree of linguistic distance involved here is a short list of Franco-Provençal words with their French equivalents:

French	Franco-Provençal	
chat	tha [with *th* as in English *think*]	cat
quoi	ka	what
deux	dou	two
quatre	katro	four
arbre	obro	tree
pied	pia	foot
jaune	thona [with *th* as in English *this*]	yellow
neige	na	snow
plume	ploma	pen
grande	granta	big

free variation Variation in language which is not subject to any **constraints**. Most sociolinguists believe that variation of this type is rather rare.

Frisian A group of minority languages (see **linguistic minority**) from the **West Germanic dialect continuum**. West Frisian is spoken in the northern part of the Netherlands by about 300,000 people. North Frisian is spoken in eastern coastal areas of Schleswig-Holstein, Germany by about 10,000 people. East Frisian, which is moribund, is spoken in a small area of Ostfriesland, Germany. They are historically closely related but no longer mutually intelligible.

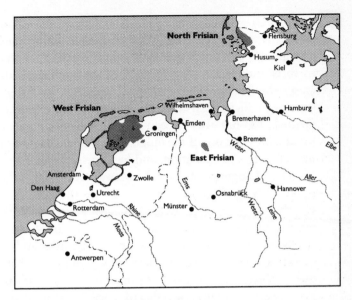

The Frisian-speaking areas

Friulian A **Rhaeto-Romance** language, related to **Romansh** and **Ladin,** from the **West Romance dialect continuum,** spoken by a **linguistic minority** of about 500,000 people in north-eastern Italy.

Fronteiriço see **Fronterizo**

Fronterizo A linguistic variety which is a mixture of Spanish and Portuguese, and which is spoken in areas of northern **hispanophone** Uruguay close to the frontier with **luso-phone** Brazil.

functional sociolinguistics A form of functional linguistics developed by Michael Halliday and his associates in which there is a particular concentration on the ways in which meaning is developed in discourse, and on **register** and **genre**.

G

Galician A language from the **West Romance dialect continuum** spoken in north-western Spain by perhaps as many as three million people. As an **Ausbau language** with a close relationship with the national language, Spanish, the status of Galician as a language, as opposed to a dialect of Spanish, has not always been secure. **Autonomy** today is signalled by the use of the language in the media and to a limited extent in education, and by the establishment of a Galician Language Academy. Many people in Galicia speak only Spanish. Those who do speak Galician are mostly bilingual in the two languages, and considerable mixing between the two may occur. Galician is linguistically closer to Portuguese than to Spanish, and has therefore been claimed by some to be a dialect of Portuguese. Historically, it would be more accurate to say that Portuguese is a dialect of Galician, since Romance dialects spread southwards from Galicia into what is now Portugal during the medieval reconquest from the Arabs.

gayspeak A label sometimes used to refer to the **antilanguage** of male homosexuals. In a number of anglophone areas, this variety includes a number of elements of **Polari** vocabulary and **backslang**.

Geechee see **Gullah**

genderlect A **variety** or **lect** which is specific to or particularly associated with either male or female speakers. This term is in most usages misleading, in that it suggests that there may be communities where male and female speakers use radically different varieties. In fact, while there are some more-or-less gender-specific usages in many if not most languages, these range from the use of a small number of words, phrases or conversational devices in some languages to particular vowels, consonants or grammatical endings in others. Most differences between male and female speech are quantitatively-revealed tendencies rather than absolute differences.

generic pronoun In linguistics, a generic form is one which refers to a class or group of entities rather than to a specific member of a class. A particular issue in recent discussion about language and society has been the generic use of the English masculine pronouns *he*, *him* and *his* (and similar pronouns in certain other languages) to include both male and female referents, as in *Any student who fails to complete his work* . . . where students may be either male or female. Feminine pronouns have traditionally not been employed in this generic way, with *she*, *her*, *hers* referring only to female persons. This apparent bias in favour of males can be awkward, illogical or misleading, and it has been argued that the generic use of *he* is unjust and undesirable in societies which believe in the equality of men and women. Linguistic solutions have been sought to the problem, such as the use of the already well-established singular *they* in English (*Any student who fails to complete their work* . . .), the use of written *s/he*, the use of generic *she*, or the invention of totally new pronoun forms.

genre An identifiably distinct type of discourse or text recognised by a particular culture and with particular linguistic characteristics. Examples of genres include poems, conversations, speeches, stories, advertisements, love letters, sermons, fairy tales, jokes, football commentaries. There is some overlap in technical usage between genre and **register**.

geographical linguistics see **geolinguistics**

geography of language see **geolinguistics**

geolinguistics (1) A relatively recent label used by some linguists to refer to work in **sociolinguistics** which represents a synthesis of Labovian **secular linguistics** and spatial **dialectology**. The quantitative study of the geographical diffusion of words or pronunciations from one area to another is an example of work in this field. (2) A term used by human geographers to describe modern quantitative research on geographical aspects of **language maintenance** and **language shift**, and other aspects of the spatial relationships to be found between languages and dialects. An example of such work is the study of geographical patterning in the use of English and Welsh in Wales. Given the model of the distinction between **sociolinguistics** and the **sociology of language**, it might be better to refer to this sort of work as the geography of language.

Geordie An informal term referring to inhabitants of the Tyneside area of north-eastern England, and hence to the English dialect and accent of that area.

Giles, Howard /dʒailz/ See **accommodation, ethnolinguistic vitality, matched guise technique**

glossolalia 'Speaking in tongues'. A religious practice associated particularly with branches of the Pentecostal Christian Church in which speakers believe that they are speaking in a language unknown to them. Research has shown that they are in fact not speaking any genuine language.

glottal stop A consonantal articulation achieved by a complete closure of the glottis followed by an audible release of this closure. This articulation has been much investigated in sociolinguistic studies of British English, in many varieties of which **t-glottaling** is a **linguistic variable**. In these varieties the glottal stop is a way of pronouncing **intervocalic** /t/, as in *city* (sometimes represented in writing as *ci'y*) and word-final /t/, as in *sit*.

graphisation A term from **language planning** used to describe that part of the process of **language development** which involves the selection of a writing system or alphabet for a language and the agreement on conventions for its orthography or spelling and punctuation. The development of an orthography usually follows on from phonological analysis carried out by linguists.

Grice, Paul see **conversational implicature, conversational maxims, cooperative principle**

Gullah /gʌlə/ A creole language with English as its major **lexifier** spoken in the United States in coastal areas, particularly off-shore islands, from southern North Carolina down to northern Florida, with a particular concentration in South Carolina and Georgia. Also known as Sea Island Creole English and Geechee. A closely related variety known as Afro-Seminole, discovered by the British sociolinguist Ian Hancock, is spoken in Bracketville, Texas.

Gumperz, John /ˈgʌmpərz/ see **Hemnesberget, institutional linguistics, Kupwar**

H

Halliday, Michael see **antilanguage, cline, functional sociolinguistics, register**

Hammer, The see **Belfast**

Hancock, Ian see **Angloromany, Gullah**

Haugen, Einar /haugn/ see **autonomy, heteronomy**

Hemnesberget /'hemnesbærgə/ A small town in northern Norway, to the south of Mo i Rana, with a current population of about 1300. The town was the site of an influential and much-quoted 1960s study of **code-switching** (between the local dialect and **Bokmål**) by John Gumperz. In spite of its sociolinguistic-theoretical importance and its insights into the functions of code-switching, the study has been criticised by Norwegian linguists, who find some aspects of the study suspect, especially because it is very usual in Norway for people to speak their local dialects on all occasions.

heteronomy A term associated with the work of the Norwegian-American linguist Einar Haugen. Dependence – the opposite of **autonomy**. Heteronomy is a characteristic of a **variety** of a **language** that has not been subject to **standardisation**, and which is not regarded as having an existence independent of a corresponding autonomous standard. A heteronomous variety is typically a nonstandard variety whose speakers and writers are socially, culturally and educationally dependent on an autonomous variety of the same language, and who look to the standard autonomous variety as the one which naturally corresponds to their **vernacular**.

Hiberno-English see **Irish English**

High variety see **diglossia**

hispanophone Spanish-speaking

historicity A characteristic of a language or language variety where there is a continuous tradition of native speakers handing down the language from one generation to another. Languages which do not have this social characteristic include artificial languages such as Esperanto; **classical languages**, such as Latin and Sanskrit, which no longer have native speakers; and **pidgin** languages, which do not (yet) have any native speakers.

Hymes, Dell see **communicative competence, ethnography of speaking, speech act**

hyperadaptation A linguistic process resulting from **dialect contact**. Speakers of one **variety** attempt to adopt features from another variety, but overdo it, overgeneralising from correspondences they have noticed between the two varieties. Thus speakers of non-rhotic English English accents, in attempting to imitate **rhotic** (for example American) **accents**, may incorrectly insert an *r* into the pronunciation of words like *calm* /ka:m/ > /ka:rm/ because they have observed that rhotic accents have an *r* in words like *farm* /fa:rm/ corresponding to their own pronunciation /fa:m/. The best known term relating to types of hyperadaptation is **hypercorrection**. Other forms include **hyperdialectism**; and hyperurbanism, in which speakers of rural dialects overgeneralise urban dialect forms. Linguistically, this process is the same as that which in child language studies and second language learning is called overgeneralisation.

hypercorrection A form of **hyperadaptation** in which speakers of a lower prestige variety, in attempting to adopt features of a higher prestige variety, incorrectly analyse differences between the two varieties and overgeneralise on the basis of observed correspondences. An example from English English is the faulty 'correction' of the north of England pronunciation of words such as *look* from /luk/ to supposedly **RP** /lʌk/ by analogy with correctly observed northern versus RP correspondences such as *duck* /duk/ versus /dʌk/. See also **Labov-hypercorrection.**)

hyperdialectism A form of **hyperadaptation** in which speakers produce overgeneralised forms in nonstandard dialects. This can take place as a result of faulty analyses, for example, in the speech of actors attempting to imitate certain regional varieties, and even in the speech of local-dialect speakers themselves if they attempt to reproduce pronunciations or constructions typical of older forms of the dialect with which they are not sufficiently familiar. It can also occur as the result of **neighbour opposition,** when dialect speakers overgeneralise differences between their own and neighbouring dialects in order to symbolise their separate identities.

hyperurbanism see **hyperadaptation**

hypocoristic A term used to refer to a 'pet name' – a familiar form of a name, such as *Bob* from *Robert*, and often involving a **diminutive,** such as *Johnny* from *John*.

I

idiolect A variety of language used by an individual speaker.

illocutionary act see **speech act theory**

illocutionary force see **speech act theory**

immersion programmes An educational system whereby pupils are taught some or all of their school subjects through the medium of a language which is not their native language. In Canada, for example, some **anglophone** children attend schools where much of the curriculum is taught in French, though they will normally continue to speak English to each other outside the classroom. The motivation is not only that children should learn to become fluent in French, but also that they should gain insights into the culture of the **francophone linguistic minority** in Canada. Compare **submersion**.

immigrant language A language spoken by a **linguistic minority** where that minority consists of a community which has only relatively recently arrived in the country in question, such as Albanian in Switzerland, Cambodian in the United States, Arabic in France, or Panjabi in the United Kingdom. Children speaking such languages are often subjected to language **submersion** in the education system of their new country. It has also been suggested, controversially, that in some cases they may suffer from double **semilingualism**.

implicational scale A term from **variation theory** particularly associated with the study of the **post-creole continuum**. The American linguist David DeCamp in 1971 introduced the **implicational table** or scalogram as a way of showing relationships between linguistic varieties. He demonstrated that certain linguistic forms from the Jamaican social dialect continuum had both **creole** and **standard** variants. These variants can be ranked in terms of their 'creoleness' and 'standardness' on an implicational hierarchy that is observed by (nearly all) speakers, such that usage by a speaker of creole forms from a particular point on the hierarchy *implies* that one can predict that he or she will also use creole forms from lower down on the hierarchy, but not necessarily from higher up.

That is, some mesolectal forms are more basilectal or acrolectal than others. Similarly, use of standard forms from a particular point on the continuum also implies use of standard forms from higher up on the hierarchy, but not necessarily use of those from lower down. See also **lect**.

implicational table A table used to portray implicational relationships, such as those obtaining on a **post-creole** or other social dialect continuum, between speakers' use of linguistic features, in which variants can be ranged on an **implicational scale**, as in the table below.

Speaker	Feature				
	1	2	3	4	5
A	Standard	Standard	Standard	Standard	Standard
B	Standard	Standard	Standard	Standard	Creole
C	Standard	Standard	Standard	Creole	Creole
D	Standard	Standard	Creole	Creole	Creole
E	Standard	Creole	Creole	Creole	Creole
F	Creole	Creole	Creole	Creole	Creole

impoverishment see **reduction**

indicator In **secular linguistics**, a **linguistic variable** which shows **social stratification** but not **style stratification**. In investigations of the **embedding problem** associated with linguistic change, indicators represent a relatively early stage in the development of linguistic variables, and may later on develop into **markers**. Indicators are typically involved in **change from below**.

indirectness A term particularly associated with **conversation analysis**, **interactional sociolinguistics** and the **ethnography of speaking**. It is normal in all human societies for speakers not always to say exactly what they mean. It is important for reasons relating to **face** and **negative** and **positive politeness** that speakers should on some occasions be able to hint at their meanings rather than stating them directly. The American sociolinguist Deborah Tannen has argued that some societies use this sort of indirectness as a conversational strategy more frequently than others. In communities such as Greece, where indirectness is rather frequently employed, speakers will thus be more sensitive to hints and clues as to what other speakers' true intentions and feeling are than in, for example, many English-speaking cultures. She has also suggested that American men use indirectness less, and are therefore less sensitive to its use by others, than American women. See also **signifying**.

informant A native speaker of a language who helps a linguist by working as a source of linguistic data from or about that language. The Linguistic Society of America has suggested that the term *consultant* should be used instead as a way of indicating that the relationship is one where the informant is the expert and the linguist the 'learner'. It is probable, however, that this suggestion was also motivated by the fact that, in American English, *informant* can also refer to someone who gives information against another person, typically a criminal. Most writers in English outside the United States continue to use *informant*, however, probably because in British English *informant* does not have this other meaning (*informer* being used instead). Informant also seems more appropriate for use in cases where the person concerned provides data without knowing that they have done so. It is perfectly possible, for example, to obtain data from writing by, or recordings of, speakers after they are dead.

inherent variability A term from **secular linguistics** which is employed to claim that variability in a particular **language variety** is not the result of the **borrowing** of additional variants from other varieties but is inherent in the system of the variety itself. While it is acknowledged that borrowing from other varieties does occur, it is also agreed by sociolinguists that all dialects of all languages are inherently variable to some extent: variability is a universal characteristic of human language. Variability may be related to an ongoing linguistic change, with variation occurring between older and newer forms, but this is not necessarily the case. Many varieties of British English, for example, show inherent variability in alternation between /h/ and Ø in words such as *hat, house* and *hedge* (see **linguistic variable**) which is not involved in any current linguistic change at all.

institutional linguistics A form of linguistics which looks at the use of language in professions such as law and medicine.

institutionalised see **foreigner talk, lingua franca**

intellectualisation The process in **language planning** in which the vocabulary of the **language** of a community is expanded, either by **borrowing** from other languages or by coining, compounding or other language-internal means. Intellectualisation is undertaken in order to enable a language's speakers more readily to speak and write about academic, scientific and other topics which the community has hitherto not spoken or written about, or which it has spoken and written about using some other language.

interactional sociolinguistics A term associated with the work of John Gumperz. A form of **micro-sociolinguistics** which studies the use of language in **face-to-face interaction** and which assumes that language as it is used in social inter-action is constitutive of social relationships i.e. speakers and listeners use language to maintain, develop, alter, refine and define social relationships.

interference see **admixture**

interlanguage A term introduced by Larry Selinker in 1972 to refer to the variety of language used by someone who is learning a foreign language. This variety is in some ways intermediate between the speaker's native language and the **target language**, since the target language will be subject to interference or **admixture** from the learner's native language. Crucially, though, the interlanguage will also contain elements which are not present in either the native language or the target language. The interlanguage will develop and change as the learner progresses, but may also be subject to **fossilisation**.

international language A **lingua franca** which is used for communication between different countries. English is currently very often used this way, as are other languages such as Russian and French.

intervocalic 'Vocalic' means 'having to do with vowels', so intervocalic is a term which is used to refer to sounds (normally consonants) which occur 'between vowels'. Intervocalic /t/ in English is thus the /t/ which appears in words like *city*, *butter*, *meeting*. In some accents of English, intervocalic /t/ may be pronounced as a **glottal stop**.

intrusive /r/ In **non-rhotic** accents of English, **non-prevocalic** /r/ does not occur. This is because a sound change has taken place in these accents such that /r/ was lost except where it occurred before a vowel. This has the consequence that words like *car* have two pronunciations, one with /r/, /ka:r/, before a vowel, as in *car engine*, and one without /r/, /ka:/, before a consonant, as in *car wash*. (Where the /r/ is pronounced, as in *car engine*, it is known as linking /r/, because it 'links' one word to the next.) This alternation between the two different pronunciations has, as a result of analogy, been extended by speakers of non-rhotic accents to words which did not originally have an /r/, as in *Ma was* /ma:/ but *Ma is* /ma:r/. It is this non-historical /r/ which is known as 'intrusive' /r/. In fact, although they are **diachronically** different, linking /r/ and intrusive /r/ are **synchronically** the same phenomenon: speakers simply automatically insert an /r/ at the end of words after the vowels of words such as *Ma, car, law, more, hear, idea, butter, America* if the next word begins with a vowel, regardless of whether this /r/ is historically 'justified' or not.

Irish English The English of Ireland (as opposed to England, Australia and so on). Sometimes less happily known as 'Hiberno-English' and, even less happily, as 'Anglo-Irish'.

isogloss A term from **dialectology** for a line drawn on a dialect map marking off an area which has one particular variant of a linguistic form from another neighbouring area which has a different variant. An additional term, isophone, is available in strict usage for referring to lines drawn between areas which have different phonetic or phonological variants, leaving isogloss to refer to lexical differences. In practice, however, most writers use isogloss to apply to phonetic, phonological, grammatical *and* lexical boundaries. Well-known isoglosses include the *maken–machen* line in Germany (see **Rhenish Fan**), the *path* /pæθ/–/pa:θ/ line in England, and the *greasy* /s/–/z/ line in the USA.

isophone see **isogloss**

J

Jamaican Creole The English-**lexifier creole** spoken in various **mesolect** and **basilect** forms in Jamaica. Jamaica provides a good example of a **post-creole continuum**. The more basilectal varieties of the creole are not readily mutually intelligible with English. The creole is often referred to in Jamaica itself as 'patwa' (see **patois**).

jargon (1) A form of **language** which has arisen in a **language contact** situation as a result of **pidginisation,** but which has not yet undergone **stabilisation** or focusing (see **focused**) or any form of even informal **codification**. Such **diffuse** language varieties are also known as pre-pidgin **varieties.** (2) A non-technical term used of the **register** associated with a particular activity by outsiders who do not participate in this activity. The use of this term implies that one considers the vocabulary of the register in question to be unnecessarily difficult and obscure. The register of law may be referred to as 'legal jargon' by non-lawyers.

jocks and burnouts see **Belten High**

Judaeo-German see **Yiddish**

Judaeo-Spanish see **Ladino**

K

Karelian A Finno-Ugric language spoken in Russia, in areas close to Finland, by about 100,000 people. It has an **Ausbau** linguistic relationship with Finnish, and has been considered by some people at some times to be a dialect of Finnish.

Kashubian A language which is spoken by a small **linguistic minority** of a few thousand people on the **North Slavic**

dialect continuum, in a small area of northern Poland to the west of Gdansk (Danzig) and Gdynia. As a language with an **Ausbau** relationship with the national language Polish, it has not always been recognised as a language in its own right as opposed to a dialect of Polish.

kernel area see **focal area**

kinship terminology Terms used to label the family relationships in human society. All human societies have the same family relationships, contracted through birth and marriage, in common. Different societies, however, group these relationships together and label them in linguistically different ways. The study of the words used to label such relationships in different societies is thus of both semantic and anthropological interest. English-speaking people do not distinguish linguistically between *uncle* 'father's brother', 'mother's brother', 'father's sister's husband' and 'mother's sister's husband'. Certain other languages do distinguish between all or some of these different relationships, and/or group them together with other relationships which in English are separate from *uncle*: 'father' and 'father's brother' may share the same term, for instance. The assumption is that this differential linguistic labelling reflects differences in the structures of different societies and in the roles and behaviour which are expected of individuals having particular relationships with one another.

Kituba A **creole** based on the Bantu language Kikongo as **lexifier**, widely spoken in the Democratic Republic of Congo, where it also has a role as a **lingua franca**. It provides a useful counterexample to the erroneous notion that all creoles have European languages as lexifiers.

Kloss, Heinz see **Abstand language, Ausbau language**

Knudsen, Knud see **Bokmål**

koiné A linguistic variety which has grown up in a **dialect contact** situation as a result of koinéisation. The process of koinéisation consists of **dialect mixture** together with or followed by the processes of **levelling** and **simplification**. The word 'koiné' is the Ancient Greek word for 'common'. Urban dialects are often koinés based on a mixture of original rural dialects. Standard languages may also be varieties that have undergone certain amounts of koinéisation.

koinéisation see **koiné, simplification, traditional dialect**

Krio A creole language with English as its **lexifier** spoken natively in Freetown, the capital of Sierra Leone, West Africa, by about half a million people, and by several million second-language users in the country as a whole as a **lingua franca**. People who have Krio as their native language are mostly descended from slaves who were repatriated from Jamaica and elsewhere in the Western Hemisphere, and the language bears a number of similarities to **Jamaican Creole**.

Kriol A creole language with English as its **lexifier** spoken natively in Australia by about 10,000 aboriginal people in northern areas of Western Australia, Northern Territory and Queensland, and by even more second-language speakers. The name Bamyili Creole is sometimes used to refer to certain dialects. Here is a version of the Lord's Prayer in Kriol (note that *melabat* translates as 'we'):

> Dedi langa hebin, yu neim im brabli haibala,
> en melabat nomo wandim enibodi garra yusum yu neim
>   nogudbalawei.

Melabat wandim yu garra kaman en jidan bos langa
melabat.
Melabat askim yu blanga gibit melabat daga blanga
dagat tudei.
Melabat bin larramgo fri detlot pipul hubin dumbat
nogudbala ting langa melabat,
en melabat askim yu blanga larramgo melabat fri du.
Melabat askim yu nomo blanga larram enijing
testimbat melabat brabli adbalawei.

Kupwar A village in India situated at the point where the
Dravidian and the Indo-European language families meet.
The two languages of the area are Kannada (Dravidian)
and Marathi (Indo-European). Research by John Gumperz showed that centuries of intense **language contact**
between the two languages has led to considerable linguistic convergence, with the two languages as spoken in
the village having common sentence structures, word-
structures and sound structures, and now differing mainly
in vocabulary.

Kweyol A name used to refer to the French-**lexifier** creole
varieties spoken in the Caribbean area, and particularly to
the Lesser Antillean French Creoles of St Lucia, Dominica,
Grenada, Guadeloupe, Martinique, and Trinidad and
Tobago.

$\boxed{\text{L}}$

Labov, William see **actuation problem, African American
Vernacular English, Ann Arbor case, apparent-time studies, curvilinear principle, Labov-hypercorrection, Labovian sociolinguistics, linguistic gratuity, Lower East Side,
Martha's Vineyard, principle of accountability.**

Labov-hypercorrection A secular linguistic term associated with the **embedding problem** in which **style stratification** of **markers** is such that (usually) the second highest status group in a **speech community** uses higher-status variants in formal styles more frequently than the highest status group. This linguistic behaviour can be interpreted as being the result of **linguistic insecurity**. Labov-hypercorrection should be distinguished from **hypercorrection**, which is a feature of the speech of individuals. Labov-hypercorrection is a term which is due to the British linguist J. C. Wells, who suggested that it was necessary to distinguish terminologically between individual hypercorrection and group hypercorrection of the type first described by William Labov in his research in New York City.

Labovian sociolinguistics Another term for **secular linguistics**. The American linguist William Labov is the leading figure in this field and pioneered work of this type, notably in his 1966 publication *The social stratification of English in New York City*.

Ladin A **Rhaeto-Romance** language, related to **Romansh** and **Friuian**, from the **West Romance dialect continuum**, spoken by a **linguistic minority** of about 30,000 people in the Dolomite area of northern Italy.

Ladino A language, also known as Judaeo-Spanish (in Spanish *judeoespañol*) which is spoken by the descendants of Jewish people who were expelled from Spain in 1492 and Portugal in 1497. Many of these Jews fled to the Ottoman Empire, and until the Second World War the language was widely spoken in urban areas of the Balkans, such as Thessaloniki (Greece), Sarajevo (Bosnia), Bucarest (Romania) and Sofia (Bulgaria). Most of these communities were exterminated by the Nazis, however, with the result that the language survived strongly only in Turkey, notably in Istanbul. It was also spoken in North Africa, from which it has now mostly disappeared. Ladino is essentially a form of Spanish, but with some archaisms and independent innovations, and, as with **Yiddish**, Jewish cultural and religious vocabulary derived from Hebrew, plus many borrowings from Greek and Turkish (or, in North Africa, French and Arabic). The language is still spoken in Istanbul, Israel, the USA, and elsewhere, but does not appear to have much **ethnolinguistic vitality**. It has been written both in the Hebrew and in the Latin alphabet.

Lallans A name, meaning 'Lowlands', often used to refer to literary varieties of **Scots**.

lame A term introduced into **sociolinguistics** from **African American Vernacular English** by William Labov, and now used as a technical term to describe individuals who are 'outsiders' or only peripheral members of a particular **social network** or **peer group**. It is believed that the linguistic behaviour of lames is less regular, because it is less subject to focusing (see **focused**) than that of core members of a group. Labov also points out that academic linguists typically are – or have become – lames, and that their intuitions about their own original dialects may therefore be somewhat unreliable.

Landsmål see **Nynorsk**

language Not only a linguistic, but also a political, cultural, social and historical term. An **Ausbau**-type language is a collection of linguistic varieties which consists of an autonomous variety, together with all the varieties that are heteronomous (dependent) on it. Whether or not a group of varieties form an Ausbau type of language will be doubtful, or impossible to determine, where none of the varieties is autonomous. This will also be difficult in situations where the nature or direction of heteronomy is a matter of political or cultural dispute. There are thus disagreements as to whether Serbo-Croat is one or two languages (see **polycentric standard**); whether Macedonian is a language in its own right or a dialect of Bulgarian; whether Sami (Lappish) is one language or six, and so on. **Abstand**-type languages can be considered languages for purely linguistic reasons.

language attitudes The attitudes which people have towards different **languages, dialects, accents** and their speakers. Such attitudes may range from very favourable to very unfavourable, and may be manifested in subjective judgements about the 'correctness', worth and aesthetic qualities of varieties, as well as about the personal qualities of their speakers. Linguistics has shown that such attitudes have no linguistic basis. Sociolinguistics notes that such attitudes are social in origin, but that they may have important effects on language behaviour, being involved in **acts of identity**, and on linguistic change (see **linguistic insecurity**). Language attitudes is one of the most important topics in the **social psychology of language**.

language conflict In multilingual situations, social strife and other problems which arise where the needs or rights or wishes of different groups speaking different languages conflict. The term is more especially applied to disagreements that are specifically to do with language, such as which language is to be the official language in a particular area; which language children are to receive their education in; and which language is to be used in the courts. Belgium has a history of language conflict, with disagreements

concerning language-use rights between its Dutch-, French-
and German-speaking populations flaring up from time to
time. **Language planning** activities are often directed at
solving problems arising out of language conflict.

language contact A term used to apply to situations where
two or more groups of speakers who do not have a native
language in common are in social contact with one another or come into such contact. Communication between
the groups may be difficult in the short term, and may in
the long term lead to the different languages influencing
one another, as a result of **bilingualism** on the part of
(some of) the speakers involved. Language contact may
lead to or involve phenomena such as **borrowing, code-
switching, language shift, lingua francas, multilingualism**
and **pidginisation.** See also **dialect contact.**

language cultivation A term often used to translate Scandinavian *språkvård*. Its meaning is roughly equivalent to
language development or **corpus planning,** but it is also
concerned, as they are not, with notions such as **correctness** and literary style.

language death In situations of **multilingualism** and **language
contact, language shift** may take place, particularly on the
part of **linguistic minority** groups. If the entire community
shifts totally to a new language, the original language will
eventually have no speakers left in the community in
question, and the end point of the process of language
shift will be language death. Some writers distinguish
between situations of language loss, where total shift
occurs in only one of the communities speaking the
language, such as the loss of Dutch in immigrant communities in Australia; and language death, which is the
total loss of a language from the world, when all the

speakers of a language shift, as with the loss of Manx on the Isle of Man. We can also distinguish language murder, when a language dies out as a result of genocide, as in the case of Tasmanian. See also **language endangerment**.

language deficit see **verbal deprivation**

language determination A term from **language planning** not significantly different in its usage from **status planning**.

language development In **language planning**, language development consists of the processes of **graphisation, standardisation** and **intellectualisation**. See also **corpus planning**.

language endangerment A situation in which a language is in danger of undergoing **language death**.

language intertwining A term developed by the Dutch linguist Peter Bakker to refer to a rare type of language which results from very intense and intimate contact between two languages, resulting in a mixture of both languages in about equal proportions. Examples of such languages are **Copper Island Aleut** and **Michif**.

language loss see **language death**

language loyalty Positive **language attitudes** towards their native language which lead individuals and communities to keep on speaking this language and to pass it on to their children, thereby achieving **language maintenance** rather than **language shift**.

language maintenance The opposite of **language shift** and **language death**. Where language maintenance occurs, a community of speakers continues speaking its original language, rather than shifting to some other language. The term is used most frequently of **linguistic minority** communities, since these are most likely to experience language shift. Many minority language communities attempt to secure language maintenance through various **language planning** activities, such as obtaining a role for the minority language in education.

language missionary A person who has a much greater role in influencing the course of linguistic change in a community than one would normally expect to be the case for a particular individual. Such individuals will usually be people who for some reason are respected and accepted as insiders by members of the community, but who differ from the other members of the community in their linguistic characteristics. The term was originally used by the Norwegian dialectologist Anders Steinsholt, but is now used by scholars working on the diffusion of linguistic changes in many parts of the world. Steinsholt described the strong linguistic influence exerted on a southern Norwegian rural community by small numbers of local men who had been away from the community on whaling expeditions and who later returned, bringing with them new non-local dialect forms they had acquired from other whalers.

language murder see **language death**

language myths Things which are widely believed by non-linguists to be true about language or languages but which are actually not, such as the widespread belief that some languages are more 'primitive' than others, or that language change ought to be, and can be, stopped. See also **folk linguistics**.

language planning Activities carried out by governmental, official or other influential bodies that are aimed at establishing which language varieties are used in a particular community, and subsequently at directing or influencing which language varieties are to be used for which purposes in that particular community, and what the linguistic characteristics of those varieties are to be. Language planning is normally undertaken in order to improve communications and education, and/or influence **nationism** and/or achieve **language maintenance**. Language planning can be divided into two main types of activity, often labelled respectively **language determination** or **status planning**, and **language development** or **corpus planning**. See also **language cultivation**.

language revitalisation see **language revival**

language revival If, as a result of the process of **language shift**, a language is in danger of **language death**, attempts can be made to reverse this process. Such attempts can be called 'reversing language shift' and are carried out by means of language revitalisation programmes. The term language revival is most often used to refer to attempts to reverse language shift when it is already complete, that is, when the language is dead, or almost so. The best known and perhaps only successful example of language revival is provided by the case of Hebrew, which was for many centuries a **classical** liturgical language with no native speakers but which is now the native language of several million people in Israel.

language shift The opposite of **language maintenance**. The process whereby a community (often a **linguistic minority**) gradually abandons its original language and, via a (sometimes lengthy) stage of **bilingualism**, shifts to another language. For example, between the seventeenth and twentieth centuries, Ireland shifted from being almost entirely Irish-speaking to being almost entirely English-speaking. Shift most often takes place gradually, and **domain** by domain, with the original language being retained longest in informal family-type contexts. The ultimate end-point of language shift is **language death**. The process of language shift may be accompanied by certain interesting linguistic developments such as **reduction** and **simplification**.

language use see **elaborated code, restricted code**

Lappish see **Sami**

Latino A term used by Americans to refer to **hispanophone** people living in the USA. The feminine form is Latina.

lect Another term for **variety** or 'kind of language' which is neutral with respect to whether the variety is a **sociolect** or a (geographical) **dialect**. The term was coined by the American linguist Charles-James Bailey who, as part of his work in **variation theory**, has been particularly interested in the arrangement of lects in **implicational tables**, and the diffusion of linguistic changes from one linguistic environment to another and one lect to another. He has also been particularly concerned to define lects in terms of their linguistic characteristics rather than their geographical or social origins.

Le Page, Robert see **acts of identity, diffuse, diffusion, focused**

levelling One of the linguistic processes which may take place in a situation of **dialect mixture** and which can lead, together with **simplification**, to the development of a

koiné. Levelling refers to the process whereby the number of variant pronunciations, words or grammatical forms that are present in the dialect mixture are reduced as a result of focusing (see **focused**), to a smaller number of variants, usually one. Levelling usually consists of getting rid of forms which are used by only a minority of speakers or are in some other way unusual.

lexical set A set of lexical items – words – which have something in common. In discussions of English accents, this 'something' will most usually be a vowel, or a vowel in a certain phonological context. We may therefore talk about the English 'lexical set of *bath*', meaning words such as *bath*, *path*, *pass*, *last*, *laugh*, *daft* where an original short *a* occurs before a front voiceless fricative /f/, /θ/ or /s/. The point of talking about this lexical set, rather than a particular vowel, is that in different accents of English these words have different vowels: /æ/ in the north of England and most of North America, /aː/ in the south of England, Australia, New Zealand and South Africa.

lexifier In the study of **pidgin** and **creole** languages, the language from which most of the vocabulary has been taken. In English-based Creoles, such as **Krio** and **Sranan**, there are more words that have come from English than from any other language. See also **source language**.

Lingua Franca A Romance-based **pidgin**, with **Provençal** and Italian as the main **lexifiers**, but also derived, in some areas more than others, from Portuguese, Spanish, French, Catalan and **Ladino**. Now extinct, but formerly spoken in coastal areas of the Mediterranean, including especially North Africa, the Levant and the Greek islands, as a trading **lingua franca**. Also known as 'Sabir'. It is thought by many to have been the source of **Polari**. Some scholars who favour the **monogenesis** theory of pidgin and **creole** origins have suggested that the Lingua Franca was the original pidgin from which all others are derived. The term means 'Frankish language', with 'Frank' being a label often used by the Orthodox Christian people of the eastern Mediterranean to refer to Catholics from the west, particularly if Romance-language speaking.

lingua franca A language which is used in communication between speakers who have no native language in common. For example, if English is used in communication between native speakers of Swedish and Dutch, then it is functioning as a lingua franca. Lingua francas which are used in a large-scale institutionalised way in different parts of the world include Swahili in East Africa and French and English in West Africa. A **pidgin** language is a particular form of lingua franca. The term is derived from the Mediterranean lingua franca, **Lingua Franca**.

linguistic area A geographical area, also known by the German term Sprachbund, in which long-term **language contact** has given rise to a large number of similarities between languages, even in cases where they are not historically closely related. The best-known linguistic area in Europe is the Balkans, where, amongst a number of other similarities, Albanian, Romanian, Macedonian and Bulgarian all have definite articles that are placed after the noun, unlike languages in neighbouring areas or other languages with which they are more closely related. See also **substratum**.

linguistic atlas A book consisting of dialect maps of a particular area, often showing **isoglosses**.

linguistic community see **speech community**

linguistic gratuity, principle of The principle, adumbrated by Walt Wolfram, that linguists who have obtained linguistic data from members of a speech community should actively pursue ways in which they can return linguistic favours to that community. This is very close to William Labov's 'Principle of the debt incurred', which states that a linguist who has obtained linguistic data from members of a speech community has an obligation to use the knowledge based on that data for the benefit of the community, when that community has need of it. This principle was seen at work in the operation of the **Ann Arbor** case.

linguistic insecurity A set of **language attitudes** in which speakers have negative feelings about their native variety, or certain aspects of it, and feel insecure about its value or '**correctness**'. This insecurity may lead them to attempt to **accommodate** to or acquire higher status speech forms, and may lead to **hypercorrection** on the part of individuals and **Labov-hypercorrection** on the part of social groups. Labov has suggested that it is normally the second-highest status-group in a society that is most prone to linguistic insecurity.

linguistic market A translation of the French term *marché linguistique* due to Pierre Bourdieu and employed in Canadian sociolinguistic research by Sankoff and Laberge. They argue that it is possible to account for much sociolinguistic variability in language use in terms of the extent to which speakers' economic activity requires them to be able to use standard or other prestigious forms of language. They suggest that this may be a more important factor in determining linguistic behaviour than speakers' social class or social status background. Thus a working-class hotel receptionist may speak a **sociolect** not normally thought of as being typical of working-class speakers.

linguistic minority A social group within a nation-state or other organisational unit whose native **language** is different from the language which is spoken natively by the largest number of people in that state or unit. Thus Welsh speakers constitute a linguistic minority in Britain, Dutch speakers a linguistic minority in France and Albanian speakers a linguistic minority in Greece. Some languages can be both majority languages (like German in Germany and Austria) and minority languages (like German in France and Romania). Other languages may be minority languages everywhere they are spoken, such as Sami (Lappish) in Norway, Sweden, Finland and the Soviet Union. See **exogenous minority language, endogenous minority language.**

linguistic relativity see **Sapir-Whorf hypothesis**

linguistic variable A linguistic unit, sometimes known as a sociolinguistic variable, initially developed by Labov in connection with his work in **secular linguistics** and **variation theory,** in order to be able to handle linguistic variation. Variables may be lexical and grammatical, but are most often phonological. A phonological variable may be more or less than a phoneme, but will be associated with a particular lexical set or group of words in which phonetic variation has been observed to occur, where that variation can be related to social variables or to other linguistic variables. A linguistic variable in many forms of British English is (h) – it is usual to symbolise linguistic variables by the use of parentheses – which stands for the presence or absence of /h/ in words such as *hammer, house* and *hill.* Many speakers will sometimes pronounce /h/ in words of this type and sometimes not, whereas other speakers will always pronounce it – its presence is variable. The variable (h) does not refer to /h/ at the beginning of unstressed words such as *have*, *has*, *his*, *him*, *her*, since no speaker has an /h/ in these words unless they are stressed. The variable (h) is thus said to have two variants, /h/ and Ø.

linguistic variation and change Linguistic research which is based on empirical work in **secular linguistics** and which is concerned to apply the data obtained in such studies to the solution of problems of linguistic theory, such as how and why language changes, and what is the cognitive status of linguistic variability. Work on **polylectal grammars** and **variable rules** are examples of research in variation theory. The distinction between secular linguistics and variation theory is not a particularly clear or very important one.

linking /r/ see **intrusive /r/**

loan word see **borrowing**

location see **domain**

locutionary act see **speech act theory**

loss of face see **face**

Low German A language of the **West Germanic dialect continuum** which is spoken in the northern part of Germany, also known as Plattdeutsch. It is today often considered to be a dialect of German, but it does have history of being used, particularly in the late medieval and early modern period under the Hanseatic League, as a standardised language of communication not only in Germany but also in Scandinavia and around the Baltic sea (that is, it had **autonomy**). Some idea of the nature of differences between Low German and German can be obtained from the following short list:

Low German	German	
een	ein	one
ik	ich	I
Huus	Haus	house
tain	zehn	ten
he	er	he
Foot	Fuß	foot
hebben	haben	have
maaken	machen	make
fiif	fünf	five
Süster	Schwester	sister

Low variety see **diglossia**

Lower East Side The area of Manhattan, New York City, where William Labov carried out the fieldwork for the research which was reported on in his groundbreaking 1966 book *The social stratification of English in New York City*.

lusophone Portuguese-speaking

Luxemburgish A language, until quite recently widely considered to be a dialect of German, which is spoken by about 250,000 native speakers in Luxembourg and a small neighbouring area around Arlon in Belgium. Also called Letzeburgisch. German is still the language most often used in writing in Luxembourg, but there is some literary activity in Luxemburgish. There is also an important presence of Luxemburgish in primary education, government and the media.

l-vocalisation A sound change in which the consonant /l/ turns into a high or mid vowel. In English a number of accents have undergone vocalisation of /l/ in words such as *hill* and *milk*. In Cockney, for example, *milk* is pronounced [miuk].

M

macrosociolinguistics A term sometimes used to cover **secular linguistics**, the **sociology of language** and other areas involving the study of relatively large groups of speakers. Compare **microsociolinguistics**.

marché linguistique see **linguistic market**

marker In Labovian **secular linguistics**, a **linguistic variable** which shows **social stratification** *and* **style stratification**. In investigations of the **embedding problem** associated with linguistic change, markers represent an intermediate stage in the development of linguistic variables, having developed out of **indicators**, and having the potential to become **stereotypes**. Markers are typically involved in **change from below**.

Martha's Vineyard An island off the coast of Massachusetts, USA, which was the site of the first ever study, by William Labov, in the paradigm that is now referred to as **linguistic variation and change**. This was reported on in his 1963 paper 'The social motivation of a sound change'. This can most easily be read in Labov's 1972 book *Sociolinguistic patterns*.

matched-guise technique A technique used in work in the **social psychology of language** in order to investigate **language attitudes**. The technique involves playing recordings of different speakers reading aloud the same passage of prose but using different **accents, dialects** or **languages**. Subjects are asked to listen to the recordings and to evaluate the speakers as best they can by listening to their voices on parameters such as *friendly–unfriendly, intelligent–unintelligent, reliable–unreliable* and so on. The technique is called 'matched guise' because two of the speakers listened to by the subjects are, unbeknown to them, actually the same person, appearing in two different guises, that is using two different varieties of language. The assumption then is that, if subjects evaluate this speaker differently in his or her two different guises, the difference in the evaluation cannot be due to the speaker, or to his or her voice itself, but to reactions to his or her accent, dialect or language. Work by the British social psychologist Howard Giles has found that a person speaking in an **RP** accent is evaluated as being more intelligent but less friendly than that same person speaking in a local accent. See also **subjective reaction test**.

maxims of conversation see **conversational maxims**

merger A sound change in which two forms, usually vowels or consonants, collapse into one. For example, the vowel of English *see, meet, teem* used to be distinct from the vowel of *sea, meat, team*, but now they have become merged.

mesolect In a **social dialect continuum**, the **lect** or lects which have a social status intermediate between the **acrolect** and the **basilect**. In the Jamaican **post-creole continuum**, the mesolects are the varieties which are linguistically and socially ranged on the continuum between the **Standard English** acrolect and the Jamaican **creole** basilect.

Métis see **Michif**

Michif A remarkable language which is the result of **language intertwining**. It is historically a mixture of French and the North American Algonquian language Cree, in which the verbs are mainly Cree and the nouns and adjectives and articles are mainly French. The name of the language comes from the French word *métis*, which means 'of mixed race', and indeed the speakers of Michif are an ethnic group descended for the most part from Cree women and French-Canadian men. This **ethnic group**, and the language, developed in Canada, but as a result of nineteenth-century conflicts between the Michif and the Canadian government, most of the few hundred speakers now live in North Dakota, USA. Younger people are said no longer to be learning it.

microsociolinguistics A term sometimes used to cover the study of **face-to-face interaction**, **discourse analysis**, **conversation analysis**, and other areas of **sociolinguistics** involving the study of relatively small groups of speakers. Compare **macrosociolinguistics**.

Mid-Atlantic States A term often encountered in American dialectology. The States on the eastern seaboard of the USA which lie between New England and the South, namely New York, New Jersey, Pennsylvania, Delaware, Maryland and, in some usages, Virginia. It also includes Washington DC.

Midland dialect The English dialect area in the USA which lies between the Northern and Southern dialect areas. In the east, the area includes southern New Jersey, central and southern Pennsylvania, northern Delaware and Maryland, West Virginia, western Virginia, and central and southern Ohio. Some American dialectologists dispute that there is any such area, preferring to see it as divided between the Lower North and the Upper South.

Midwest, The A geographical term used in American English dialectology to refer to the area immediately to the west of **New England** and the **Mid-Atlantic States** and to the north of **The South**. It is often considered to consist of the following states: Illinois, Indiana, Iowa, Kansas, Michigan, Minnesota, Missouri, Nebraska, North Dakota, South Dakota, Ohio and Wisconsin.

Milroy, James see **Belfast, network strength, social network**

Milroy, Lesley see **Belfast, network strength, social network**

Milton Keynes A new town in England which has been the site of a major study by Paul Kerswill into dialect mixture and the formation of a new dialect.

minority language see **linguistic minority**

Miskito Coast The Miskito Coast is the Caribbean coastal area of Nicaragua and Honduras consisting of a lowland strip about 210 miles long. The British founded the principal Miskito coast city of Bluefields (Nicaragua) and there are about 30,000 native speakers of English in this area who look to Bluefields as their centre. Most of them are of African origin. English is also spoken in many different locations on the Caribbean coast of the Miskito Coast mainland of Honduras. See **Central American English**.

Mitchif see **Michif**

modernisation see **intellectualisation**

monogenesis A term associated with the study of the world's **creole** languages and their history. Creole languages have many linguistic features in common. This is particularly true of the Atlantic creoles – those spoken on either side of the Atlantic Ocean, such as Krio in Sierra Leone, Sranan in Surinam, and Gullah in the United States. But it is also true, importantly, not only of very many creoles of English origin, but also of French-based creoles, such as Haitian Creole, and of Portuguese-based creoles. One explanation for these similarities is that the Atlantic creoles (at least) are monogenetic. That is, they are similar because they have a single common origin. They are all descended, this explanation claims, from the same **pidgin** language which was probably spoken in West Africa, where the original creole arose as a result of the slave trade, and from where it/they spread to many other parts of the world. Crucial to the monogenesis hypothesis is the **relexification** hypothesis, which explains how English, French and Portuguese creoles can all have the same origin. Like all theories of creole origins, this hypothesis is controversial. The opposite of monogenesis is **polygenesis**.

monolingual see **monolingualism**

monolingualism The opposite of **bilingualism** and **multilingualism**. A sociolinguistic situation in which only one language is involved is said to be a monolingual situation. An individual who can speak only one language is said to be 'monolingual'.

morphological transparency A term used to refer to the phenomenon whereby the meaning of a grammatical form is apparent from the meaning of its component parts. Thus, the English form *went* is not morphologically transparent, but the equivalent **Jamaican Creole** form *bin guo*, literally 'past + go', is transparent. The term is often used in the discussion of **pidgin** languages, where the phenomenon occurs frequently.

mother-in-law language see **avoidance language**

mother tongue see **native language**

multilingualism The opposite of **monolingualism**. A sociolinguistic situation in which more than one language is involved, usually involving also **language contact** and individual **bilingualism**. Note that many sociolinguists use the term 'bilingualism' to refer to individuals, even if they are trilingual, quadrilingual etc. and reserve the term 'multilingualism' for nations or societies, even if only two languages are involved.

multiple negation A feature of the grammatical structure of most dialects of English which is, however, not found in **Standard English**. In sentences such as *I can't find none nowhere* and *I don't never do nothing*, more than one – or multiple – negative forms occur, whereas the equivalent sentences in the Standard English variety contain only one negative form each: *I can't find any anywhere* and *I don't ever do anything*. Multiple negation formerly occurred in all varieties of English, but has been lost from Standard English during the last 300 years or so. Multiple negation is widely regarded as being 'incorrect', but this evaluation is simply due to the fact that it is a feature of lower status **sociolects**. It is a feature of the standard dialects of very many other languages, including French and Russian. Another name for multiple negation is negative concord, and it is also often called the double negative.

multiplex see **network strength**

Mundart see **traditional dialect**

mutual intelligibility The extent to which speakers of one variety are able to understand speakers of another variety. Mutual intelligibility may be a matter of degree – Swedish speakers can understand Norwegian more readily than they can Danish. Note too that the degree of intelligibility may not be entirely mutual – speakers of variety A may be able to understand speakers of variety B more easily than vice versa. And mutual intelligibility can also be acquired – speakers can learn to understand a variety which they initially had considerable difficulty with.

N

national language A language which functions as the main language of a nation state.

nationalism Feelings and sentiments relating to **nationality**. Nationalism is distinct from – and may in certain situations be in conflict with – practical issues concerning **nationism**. In a multilingual society such as India, nationism might suggest that a non-indigenous language such as English might be the best choice as the official language, while sentiments of nationalism might favour indigenous languages such as Hindi and Tamil.

nationality According to the American sociologist of language Joshua Fishman, a large-scale sociocultural group of people who feel themselves to be a social group distinct from other social groups. Nationality implies also that the group in question operates on a more than purely local scale. Nationality and **ethnic group** are not distinguished by all writers on **language planning** and **multilingualism**.

nationism A term used in discussions of **language planning** and **multilingualism**. According to Joshua Fishman, a nation is a political and territorial unit which is largely under the control of a particular **nationality**. Nationism, then, is a concept which has to do with the problems of administering such a political and territorial unit.

native language see **first language**

native speaker A speaker who has a language as their **first language**.

Ndjuka An English-based **creole** language i.e. a creole with English as its main **lexifier**, spoken in the interior of **Surinam** by about 15,000 people, with a small number of speakers over the border in Guyane. The language dates from about 1730 and is spoken by the descendants of escaped African slaves who maintain a culture which is in many respects a mixture of West African and Amerindian traditions. Ndjuka is a 'deep' creole i.e. because the official colonial language of the country was Dutch, Ndjuka has been little influenced by English and, unlike in the case of **Jamaican Creole**, no **post-creole continuum** has developed. See also **Sranan**.

negation see **multiple negation**

negative concord see **multiple negation**

negative face see **negative politeness, positive politeness**

negative politeness A concept derived from the sociolinguistic work of Penelope Brown and Stephen Levinson on politeness. In this approach, politeness is concerned with the actions people perform to maintain their **face** and that of the other people who they are interacting with. Positive face has to do with presenting a good image of oneself and securing the approval of others. Negative face has to do with maintaining one's freedom of action and freedom of imposition by others. Negative politeness consists of acts which are designed to preserve or restore the hearer's negative face, by expressing the speaker's reluctance to impose his or her wants on the hearer, and/or by acknowledging the social distance between the speaker and the hearer. One way of doing this would be to say something like *I don't like to bother you, but* . . .

neighbour opposition see **hyperdialectism**

network strength A concept originally employed in linguistics by the British sociolinguists James Milroy and Lesley Milroy in their research in Belfast. The strength of a **social network** depends on the degree to which it is dense and multiplex. The density of a social network depends on the degree to which the people who form the social network all know each other. The multiplexity of a social network depends on the extent to which individuals are bound to one another by more than one relationship, for example, two people might be cousins *and* friends *and* workmates.

New England A geographical term used in American English dialectology to refer to the northeastern states: Maine, Vermont, New Hampshire, Massachusetts, Connecticut, Rhode Island.

non-prevocalic /r/ The consonant /r/ in English where it occurs before a consonant, as in *start*, or before a pause, as in *star*, rather than before a vowel, as in *starry*. 'Non-prevocalic' means 'not before a vowel'. Also known, less accurately, as 'postvocalic /r/'. Accents of English differ as to whether or not they have lost non-prevocalic /r/ through linguistic change over the past 300 years or so. English accents which have retained the original pronunciation and have not lost non-prevocalic /r/ are known as **rhotic accents**.

non-rhotic accents see **rhotic accents**

nonstandard dialect In the case of languages which have undergone **standardisation**, any **dialect** other than the standard dialect or standardised variety. Such dialects are normally heteronomous with respect to the standard variety. Nonstandard varieties of English may be referred to collectively by the label **nonstandard English**.

nonstandard English Any **dialect** of English other than **Standard English**. Nonstandard dialects of English differ from Standard English most importantly at the level of grammar. Examples of widespread nonstandard grammatical forms in English include **multiple negation**, past tense *done* rather than *did*, and the use of *ain't* rather than standard *isn't*, *aren't*, *haven't* and *hasn't*. One nonstandard dialect of English that has been extensively discussed in **sociolinguistics** is **African American Vernacular English**.

Nordberg, Bengt see **Eskilstuna**

Norfolk Island see **Pitkern**

NORM An acronym introduced by the Canadian linguist J. K. Chambers to describe the sort of informants typically sought after during their fieldwork by practitioners of **traditional dialectology**. Traditional dialectologists have often concentrated on 'non-mobile older rural male' speakers of the **dialect** under study because they have believed that such speakers were the most likely to speak the local traditional dialect in a 'pure' form, uninfluenced by the standard or by other dialects.

normative see **prescriptive**

Northern Cities Shift A sound change currently under way in urban areas of the north-central and north-eastern United States, notably Milwaukee, Chicago, Detroit, Cleveland, Buffalo, Rochester and Syracuse. In this area there is a movement of the vowels of the **lexical sets** of DRESS, TRAP, LOT, STRUT, THOUGHT as illustrated in the diagram. This has the result that to people from other parts of the country, *rest* sounds like *rust*, *John* sounds like *Jan*, *cut* sounds like *caught* and *caught* sounds like *cot*.

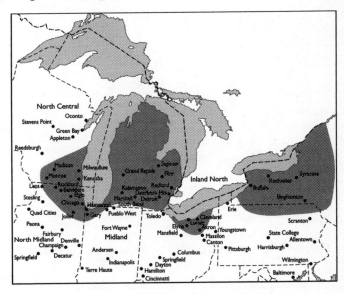

The Northern Cities Shift area

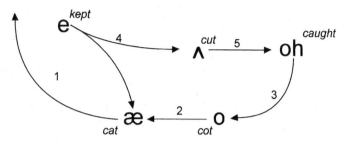

Northern Cities Shift

North Slavic dialect continuum A **dialect continuum** comprising the dialects of the East Slavic languages Russian, Ukrainian, and Belarusan, and the West Slavic languages Polish, **Kashubian**, Slovak and Czech. The transitions between Belarusan and Polish, Ukrainian and Polish, and Ukrainian and Slovak involve rather large linguistic differences, but mutual intelligibility may still be achievable.

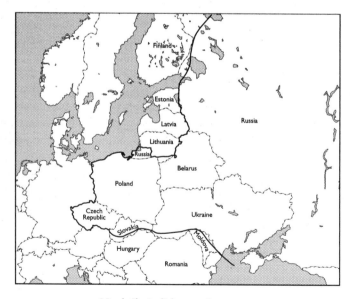

North Slavic dialect continuum

Nynorsk /nyːnɔːʃk/ One of the two officially recognised standard forms of Norwegian, the other being **Bokmål**. When Norway gained independence from Denmark in the early nineteenth century, it was felt by many that Danish should be replaced as the official language by a standardised form of the closely related Scandinavian language Norwegian. There were two conflicting solutions to the problem of devising a Norwegian standard. One, promoted by Ivar Aasen (1813–96), was to devise a whole new standard based on Norwegian dialects, particularly those of the west of the country which were least like Danish (For the other solution, see **Bokmål**.) As a result of Norwegian governmental **language planning** policies, this form of Norwegian has gradually been modified so that it is now less different from Bokmål. Originally called Landsmål 'language of the country', it is now known as Nynorsk 'new Norwegian'. See also **Ausbau language**.

O

Oakland A city in northern California with a large African American population. It received considerable attention in 1996 when the school board passed a resolution instructing that educators should recognise that **African American Vernacular English** (referred to as 'Ebonics' by the board and in the media coverage which followed) was a systematic linguistic system which differed significantly from **Standard English** to the point of being a separate language, and drawing parallels with bilingual education programmes.

Observer's Paradox A term invented by the American linguist William Labov to describe the major methodological problem of **secular linguistics**. Secular linguistic research is based on analyses of linguistic data as obtained from people using a **vernacular variety** in a natural way in everyday speech situations in the **speech community**. However, observing and recording such speech is difficult because as soon as people realise that their language is the focus of attention, they will tend to speak in a less natural and vernacular manner. The observer's paradox is thus that 'what linguists want to do is to observe the way in which people speak when they are not being observed'. A number of different methodologies have been developed to attempt to overcome this paradox (see **participant observation** and **rapid and anonymous interviews**).

Occitan A language of the **West Romance dialect continuum** which is spoken in the southern third of France (apart from the Catalan and Basque-speaking areas), as well as in Monaco and neighbouring areas of Italy. It is today sometimes considered to be a dialect of French, but the linguistic differences from French are considerable, and Occitan does have a history of being used, particularly in the late mediaval period – often under the name of Provençal - as a standardised literary language (i.e. it had **autonomy**) and as an **official language** in the area. It was revived as a literary language in the nineteenth century. Today all speakers are bilingual with French, and most speakers are found in rural areas. The main dialects are Gascon, Limousin, Auvergnat, Languedocien and Provençal. Some idea of the linguistic differences between Occitan and French can be gained from this short list:

Occitan	French	
cat	chat	cat
porta	port	door
kadena	chaîne	chain
amb	avec	with
canti	je chante	I sing
mel	miel	honey

petita	petite	small
dreit	droit	right
cambiar	changer	change
causa	chose	thing

official language A language or languages which by law must or may be used in government, law, education and other similar institutions in a particular country. Fewer than 100 of the world's approximately 6,500 languages are official languages.

onomastics The linguistic study of names, incuding place names, hydronyms (the names of lakes and rivers), family names (surnames), given names ('first names') and naming practices (such as whether and how women change their names at marriage).

optimal rules see **variable rule**

overcorrection see **hypercorrection**

overgeneralisation see **hyperadaptation**

overreporting A term used, in connection with **self report tests,** to describe claims by respondents that they use higher status or more standard linguistic forms than they actually do use, thus revealing favourable attitudes to such forms. In tests involving English speakers, female respondents have been statistically more likely to report in this way than male respondents.

Ozarks, The A hilly area of southern Missouri, northern Arkansas and north-eastern Oklahoma, USA, which has been much studied by American dialectologists because of its **traditional dialects.**

P

Pakeha A Maori word referring to New Zealanders of European origin which often appears in sociolinguistic studies comparing linguistic behaviour or characteristics of the two major ethnic groups in New Zealand.

Palenquero A **creole** language with Spanish as the **lexifier** spoken by about 2,000 speakers in the Palenque area of Columbia, South America, inland from Cartagena.

Palmerston Island Palmerston English is spoken on Palmerston Island (Polynesian *Avarau*), a coral atoll in the Cook Islands about 250 miles northwest of Rarotonga, by descendants of Cook Island Maori and English speakers. William Marsters, a ship's carpenter and cooper from Gloucestershire, England, came to uninhabited Palmerston Atoll in 1862. He had three wives, all from Penrhyn/ Tongareva in the Northern Cook Islands. He forced his wives, seventeen children and numerous grandchildren to use English all the time. Virtually the entire population of the island today descends from the patriarch. Palmerston English has some **admixture** from Polynesian but is probably best regarded as a dialectal variety of English rather than a contact language.

pandialectal Found in all dialects of a particular language.

panlectal grammar see **polylectal grammar**

Papiamentu A **creole** language with Spanish and Portuguese as the **lexifiers**. It is the majority language in the Netherlands Antilles islands of Aruba, Bonaire and Curaçao, off the north coast of South America.

parole see **langue and parole**

participant see **domain**

participant observation An anthropological technique also used for carrying out sociolinguistic research. In **sociolinguistics**, work of this type is designed to overcome the **observer's paradox**. The methodology involves the fieldworker becoming a member of the group under investigation, often over a considerable period of time, so that the group can be investigated from the inside. Research on the language used by the group can be carried out successfully because informal and long-term observation by an insider will not direct speakers' attention to their speech to an undue degree.

patois /'patwa/ A non-technical term which has two rather different meanings. Firstly, in many Caribbean communities, the local English or French-based **creole** language may be referred to by its speakers as 'patois'. Secondly, **traditional dialects** of French are often referred to by French speakers as 'patois'. The term is also used by some French and English speakers to refer to any language which does not have a written form.

patwa see **patois**

peer group A sociological term referring to a group of people that a person associates with and identifies with. Many of the peer groups studied by sociolinguists consist of teenage gangs or friendship groups, but any peer group to which speakers belong will be of importance for their linguistic behaviour, as discussed in sociolinguistic theories concerning **acts of identity** and **social networks**. **Lames** are speakers who are peripheral members of a particular peer group.

perceptual dialectogy A branch of **folk linguistics** which looks at where speakers believe dialects and dialect boundaries to be, and at their attitudes to different dialects.

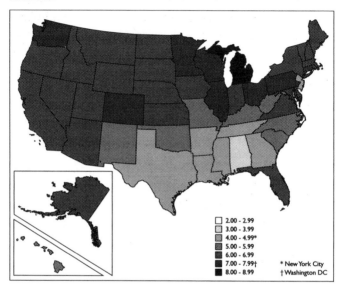

Perceptual Dialectology map (from Dennis R. Preston (ed.), *Handbook of Perceptual Dialectology*, John Benjamins Publishing Company, Amsterdam/Philadelphia 1999, p. 365)

performative An utterance in which a **speech act** is performed by a speaker simply by means of saying that they are performing it, for example 'I name this ship . . .', 'I baptise you . . .', 'I promise . . .', 'I apologise. . . '. Verbs such as 'name', 'baptise', 'promise',' apologise' are therefore known as performative verbs.

perlocutionary act see **speech act theory**

phatic communion The use of language to establish and maintain good social relations without necessarily communicating any information, such as when British people pass comments on the weather.

pidgin A variety of language without native speakers which arises in a **language contact** situation of **multilingualism**, and which operates as a **lingua franca**. Pidgins are languages which have been derived from a **source language** through **pidginisation**. The degree of pidginisation is such that **mutual intelligibility** with the source language is impossible or very difficult, and they have achieved a stable form through the processes of focusing (see **focused**) and **stabilisation**. Many well-known pidgins are derived from European source languages such as English and Portuguese, but there are also many pidgin languages which are derived from non-European sources. See also **jargon** (1) and **creole**.

pidginisation The processes of **admixture**, **reduction** and **simplification** which are associated with all imperfect adult second-language learning. Pidginisation normally leads to the development of a **jargon** (1) or **pre-pidgin** only in multilingual situations in which access to the **source language** is minimal and where pidginisation is therefore considerable. The jargon will develop into a pidgin only where there is a prolonged need for a **lingua franca** and where a stable social situation leads to focusing (see **focused**) and **stabilisation**.

Pig Latin An American schoolchildrens' **antilanguage** which consists, in its most basic form, of disguising words by taking the initial consonant or consonant cluster of a word and putting it at the end of the same word followed by the additional syllable /ei/ for example *ookbay = book*; *eetstray = street*.

Pijin Originally an English-**lexifier pidgin** language, now also a creole spoken by about 15,000 native speakers in the Solomon Islands. It is also very widely used in the country as a second language **lingua franca** by about 300,000 people. It is historically related to and rather similar to **Bislama** and **Tok Pisin**.

Pitcairn see **Pitkern**

Pitkern The language spoken on the isolated British colony of Pitcairn Island, about 2,000km south-east of Tahiti in the Pacific Ocean. The population is currently about fifty. They are descended from the mutineers on the HMS *Bounty* and their Tahitian companions. After a stay on Tahiti, the crew mutinied when their voyage to the West Indies had reached only as far as western Polynesia, and they set their captain William Bligh adrift. They returned to Tahiti, where they collected a number of local women and a few men, and, fearing discovery by the Royal Navy, sailed to Pitcairn, arriving in 1790. There, in the interests of secrecy, they burnt their ship. The island community survived undiscovered until 1808. In 1856, because of overpopulation, some of the islanders were removed to Norfolk Island, where their descendants still live. The language resembles an English-based creole and has many features of Polynesian origin. It is probably best termed an English-based **creoloid** or, because of the Polynesian contribution, 'dual source creoloid'.

Plattdeutsch see **Low German**

pluricentric language see **polycentric language**

Polari An **antilanguage** which is essentially a small amount of vocabulary, used within an English context, which is originally from Mediterranean Romance languages such as **Provençal**, Catalan and Italian. It has been argued that it is derived ultimately from the **Lingua Franca**. Some words such as *bevvy* 'drink', *lingo* 'language', *carsey* 'toilet', *manky* 'bad, poor, tasteless, unpleasant', *scarper* 'run away' have made their way into general British English slang. (Compare these words with the Italian words *bevanda* 'drink', *lingua* 'language', *casa* 'house', *mancare* 'to lack', *scappare* 'escape' – and the name of the antilanguage itself with Italian *parlare* 'speak'.) Other words such as *varda* 'look' and *lally* 'leg' are or have been associated with **gayspeak**.

polite forms see **T and V pronouns**

politeness see **negative politeness, positive politeness**

polycentric language A language in which **autonomy** is shared by two or more (usually very similar) **superposed varieties**. Examples include English (with American, English, Scottish, Australian and other standard forms); Portuguese (with Brazilian and European Portuguese standard variants); **Serbo-Croat** (with Serbian and Croatian variants) and Norwegian (with **Bokmål** and **Nynorsk**). See also **Ausbau language**.

polylectal grammar A notion associated particularly with the work of the American linguist C. J. Bailey, who argued that as speakers of a particular language are exposed, during their lifetimes, to more and more **dialects, varieties** or **lects** of that language, their increasing ability to comprehend these lects is due to their internalised knowledge or grammar of that language becoming extended to include many more lects than the one they actually speak. Linguists wanting to describe or account for this knowledge should therefore attempt to compose polylectal grammars which would reflect this competence in more than one lect. A polylectal grammar which incorporated all the varieties of a language would be a panlectal grammar.

polygenesis see **monogenesis**

Poplack, Shana see **Samaná**

popular etymology see **folk etymology**

positive face see **negative politeness; positive politeness**

positive politeness A concept derived from the sociolinguistic work of Penelope Brown and Stephen Levinson on politeness. In this approach, politeness is concerned with the actions people take to maintain their **face** and that of the other people who they are interacting with. Positive face has to do with presenting a good image of oneself and securing the approval of others. Negative face has to do with maintaining one's freedom of action and freedom of imposition by others. Positive politeness consists of acts which are designed to preserve or restore the hearer's positive face, by stressing the speaker's empathy with and social closeness to the hearer. One linguistic way of doing this would be to link the speaker and hearer together by using the pronoun forms *we*, *us* and *our*.

popular etymology see **folk etymology**

post-creole continuum A social **dialect continuum** which re- sults from **language contact** between a **creole** and its original **source language,** and consequent partial **decreo- lisation** of the creole. **Acrolects** towards the 'top' of the continuum will have been decreolised in the direction of the source language much more than **basilects** towards the bottom, with intermediate mesolectal varieties having undergone intermediate degrees of decreolisation.

post-pidgin A **language variety** which results from the partial **depidginisation** of a **pidgin** language or **jargon** (1) caused by **language contact** between it and its original **source language**.

postvocalic /r/ see **non-prevocalic /r/**

pragmatics A branch of linguistics which deals with the meaning of utterances as they occur in social contexts. Pragmatics is thus contrasted with **semantics**, which deals with purely linguistic meaning, and has connections with **discourse analysis**, **social context** and the study of **speech acts**.

pre-pidgin see **jargon** (1)

prescriptive Any set of beliefs about language which are based on the notion of **correctness** can be said to be prescriptive. The opposite of prescriptive is *descriptive*. For example, linguists typically describe languages, not as they believe they ought to be spoken, but as they are actually used by their native speakers. Linguists thus produce not *prescriptive grammars* but *descriptive grammars*. Another word for prescriptive is *normative*, since proponents of this point of view believe that norms of 'correct' usage should be adhered to. See also **folk linguistics**, **language myth**.

primary language A language which speakers use most often. (Compare **first language**.)

principle of accountability see **accountability**

principle of linguistic gratuity see **linguistic gratuity**

principle of the debt incurred see **linguistic gratuity**

proscriptive see **prescriptive**

Provençal see **Occitan**

purification The process associated with **decreolisation** and **depidginisation** in which the **admixture** which has taken place during **pidginisation** is 'repaired' as a result of **language contact** between the **creole** or **pidgin** and the **source language**. Purification thus takes the form of the exclusion of forms originally from languages other than the source language and their replacement by source language forms.

Q

quantitative paradigm see **secular linguistics**

quantitative sociolinguistics see **secular linguistics**

R

rapid and anonymous interviews One of the fieldwork techniques of **secular linguistics** designed to overcome some of the constraints of the **observer's paradox**. In this technique, the fieldworker conducts brief interviews in a public place with a large number of people in such a way as to obtain appropriate linguistic information from them without their realising that their language is being investigated and without their being unduly inconvenienced. The most famous series of such interviews was the one conducted by William Labov in which he investigated the speech of shop assistants in department stores in New York by asking questions designed to produce the response 'on the fourth floor', thus obtaining from the informants potential instances of **nonprevocalic /r/**.

real-time studies Studies of linguistic change which attempt to investigate language changes as they happen, not in **apparent time** by comparing the speech of older speakers with that of younger speakers in a given community, but in actual time, by investigating the speech of a particular community and then returning a number of years later to investigate how speech in this community has changed. In secular linguistics, two different techniques have been used in real-time studies. In the first, the same informants are used in the follow-up study as in the first study. In the second, different informants, who were too young to be included in the first study or who were not then born, are investigated in the follow-up study. One of the first linguists to use this technique was Anders Steinsholt, who carried out dialect research in the southern Norwegian community of Hedrum, near Larvik, in the late 1930s, and then returned to carry out similar research in the late 1960s.

Received Pronunciation see **RP**

reduction A part of the **pidginisation** process which occurs in **language contact** situations where imperfect adult second-language learning takes place. Reduction – or **impoverishment** – refers to the process whereby large parts of the **source language** that are available to native speakers are lost or are not acquired by pidginising non-native speakers. Comparisons between a **jargon** (1) or a **pidgin** and the source language will typically show that the source language has a larger vocabulary, and a larger repertoire of **styles**, phonological units, syntactic devices and grammatical categories. Reduction may be repaired by the process of **expansion** if **creolisation** occurs.

reduplication A process often found in **pidgin** (and therefore **creole**) languages – but also in very many other languages – in which a form is repeated in order to signal some particular semantic or grammatical category, including plurals, iteratives (forms used to indicate repetition) and **augmentatives**. For example, in **Sranan** *bigi* means 'big' while *bigibigi* means 'very big'.

register A technical term from **sociolinguistics** and particularly associated with the work of Michael Halliday which is used to describe a language **variety** that is associated with a particular topic, subject or activity. In English, registers are characterised for the most part by vocabulary, but grammatical features may also be involved. Any activity may have a specific register associated with it, whether it is football, biochemistry or flower-arranging. Well-known technical registers include those of law and medicine: the medical register uses forms such as *patella*, corresponding to non-technical *kneecap*, and *clavicle*, corresponding to *collar-bone*. Registers can identify speakers as being members of a particular **peer group**, and are for that reason often labelled **jargon** (2) by outsiders who are not part of the group in question.

relexification A hypothesis used as part of the **monogenesis** theory of the origin of **creole** languages. This theory argues that some or all of them are very similar in their structures because some or all of them are descended from the same original West African **pidgin** form of Portuguese. In order to explain how Portuguese Pidgin could have given rise to English- and French-based creoles, it is necessary to invoke the hypothesis of relexification. This holds that when speakers of the original Portuguese Pidgin came into contact with, for example, native speakers of English, their language was relexified in the direction of English, that is the grammar and phonology of their language remained the same, but the Portuguese words were gradually replaced by words from English.

restricted code A concept developed by the British sociologist Basil Bernstein in connection with his work on language use, social class and socialisation. Restricted code, originally called 'private language', is a form of language use which, according to Bernstein, is characterised by a high degree of inexplicitness and the taking of a fund of shared knowledge between speaker and hearer for granted. It is therefore not suitable for public use, Bernstein suggested, in situations where participants do not have much knowledge or many assumptions in common. Restricted code is thought of as lying at the opposite end of a continuum of types of language use from **elaborated code**. Bernstein argued that some working-class children in Britain were disadvantaged in the education system because they were able to use only restricted code. Restricted code has no connection with **nonstandard English** or any other **dialect**. It is concerned, as part of a theory of language use and social structure, with the content of what speakers say.

reversing language shift see **language revival**

Rhaeto-Romance A group of **Ausbau** languages from the West Romance dialect continuum. All of them are spoken in close geographical proximity to Italian and they have therefore sometimes been regarded, by some people, as dialects of Italian. See **Friulian, Ladin, Romansh**.

Rhenish Fan   In German dialectology, a well-known **transition zone** in the Rhineland where the major north/south **isogloss** splits into a number of different isoglosses with a fan-like configuration.

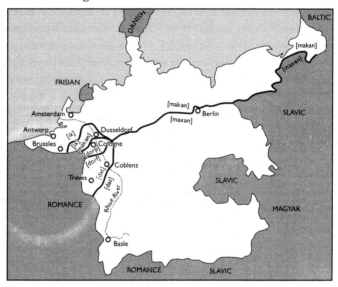

Rhenish Fan

rhotic accents   Accents of English in which **non-prevocalic** /r/ is pronounced, i.e. in which words like *star* have retained the original pronunciation /stɑr/ 'starr' rather than having the newer pronunciation /stɑː/ 'stah', where the /r/ has been lost. Rhotic accents of English include nearly all accents of Scottish and Irish English, most accents of Canadian and American English, accents from the south-west and north-west of England, some varieties of Caribbean English and a small number of New Zealand accents. Non-rhotic accents are those of Australia, South Africa, eastern and central England, some parts of the Caribbean, and a number of places on the eastern seaboard of the United States and Canada, as well as **African American Vernacular English**.

rhyming slang An form of **antilanguage**, particularly associated with the English of London, Glasgow and Australia. A word is disguised by being replaced by a short phrase which rhymes with it, and then all the words in this phrase except the first are omitted. For example, *butchers* is a shortened form of *butcher's hook* which rhymes with *look*. So *give us a butchers* means 'let me have a look'. *Whistle* means 'suit', being an abbreviated form of *whistle and flute*; *apples*, as a shortened form of *apples and pears*, means 'stairs' and *barnet*, which is short for *Barnet Fair*, means 'hair'.

Riksmål see **Bokmål**

ritual insults see **verbal duelling**

Romansh A **Rhaeto-Romance** language from the **West Romance dialect continuum** spoken by a **linguistic minority** of about 40,000 people in Switzerland and related to **Friulian** and **Ladin**. All the speakers are bilingual in Romansh and Swiss-German. The language is spoken in a number of areas, some separated from one another by German-speaking areas, of the canton of Graubünden (Romansh *Grishun*, Italian *Grigioni*, French *Grisons*) in the south-eastern part of the country. Also spelt Romansch, Romantsch.

roofing see **roofless dialects**

roofless dialects A term used mainly by German sociolinguists as a translation of German 'dachlose *Dialekte*. Roofless dialects are varieties which are not subject to Überdachung or 'roofing'. They are dialects which are linguistically **heteronomous** with respect to some autonomous **standard variety**, but which are socially and politically outside that autonomous dialect's sphere of influence. An example of this is provided by the Alsatian dialects of German which are linguistically heteronomous with respect to Standard German, but whose speakers, because they live in France, do not have full educational or other access to Standard German. See also **superposed variety**.

RP Received Pronunciation. The regionless upper-class and upper-middle-class **accent** of British – mainly English – English which is associated with the BBC and is usually taught to foreigners learning 'British' English. The label 'received' is here used in an old-fashioned sense of 'being accepted in the best social circles'. The unusual regionless nature of the RP accent is probably the result of the unusual upper-class British educational system of non-regional residential private schools, known as 'public schools'. Only a very small minority of the population of Britain – probably three to five per cent – speak in this totally regionless way.

Russenorsk A pidgin language, derived from Russian and Norwegian in about equal measure as **lexifiers**, spoken until 1917 (when the Russian Revolution disrupted trade) as a trading language in coastal northern Norway and neighbouring coastal areas of Russia. Since there were two main lexifiers, the language can be referred to as a 'dual-source pidgin'. The pidgin also contained words from English and other languages, for example:

Kak ju vil skaffom ja drikke te, davaj på sjib tvoja ligge ne jes på slipom.

'If you will eat and drink tea, please on ship your lie down and on sleep' i.e. 'If you want to eat and drink tea, please come on board your ship and lie down to sleep'

ju = you, jes = yes, slipom = sleep

S

Saami see **Sami**

Sabir see **Lingua Franca**

St Helena An English-speaking island in the South Atlantic Ocean, 1,200 miles west of Africa. The population of this British dependent territory is about 6,000. The island was discovered in 1502 by the Portuguese and the English learnt of it in 1588. It then became a port for ships travelling between Europe and the East, and in 1659 the East India Company took possession. By 1673 nearly half the inhabitants were imported slaves. Napoleon was confined on the island from 1815 until his death in 1821. The island's population is largely of mixed British, Asian and African descent. The English of St Helena is an English-**lexifier creoloid**. It has a number of **creole**-like features such as **copula deletion**, but is nevertheless obviously English.

Samaná A peninsula in the northern Dominican Republic which has a population of speakers of **African American Vernacular English**. These are the descendants of ex-slaves who settled there in the 1820s and who came mostly from New York and Philadelphia. Their English has been investigated by the linguist Shana Poplack

Sami Also known as Saami and Lappish. A Finno-Ugric language or languages related to Finnish, **Karelian** and Estonian and, much more distantly, to Hungarian and **Csángo**. It is spoken by the indigenous population of northern Norway, Sweden and Finland and adjacent areas of Russia. The bulk of the Sami people are in Norway. An interesting **Ausbau** sociolinguistic question concerns how many Sami languages there are, and what the divisions are.

The biggest Sami language or variety is Northern Sami, which centres on Karasjok and Kautokeino in northern Norway, and has about 25,000 speakers.

San Andrés and Providencia English-speaking islands about 110 miles off the coast of Nicaragua which are actually part of Colombia. The islands were settled in 1629 by English Puritans, and subsequently also by Jamaican planters and their black slaves. See **Central American English**.

Sango A **creole** language, based on the Niger-Congo language Ngbandi as the **lexifier**, which is spoken natively in the Central African Republic and widely used in this and neighbouring countries as a **lingua franca**.

Saramakkan A **creole** language spoken by about 25,000 people in the interior of **Surinam**. It is of particular interest in that, while the main **lexifier** language is English, there has also been considerable Portuguese input into the vocabulary.

Sapir-Whorf hypothesis A hypothesis associated with the American scholars Edward Sapir and Benjamin Lee Whorf, also known as the linguistic relativity hypothesis. The hypothesis suggests that people's habitual thought patterns and ways of perceiving the world are conditioned to a certain extent by the categories and distinctions that are available to them in their native language. Speakers of different languages may therefore have rather different world-views, depending on how different the languages are from one another semantically and grammatically.

Scots The language, now often regarded as having a relationship of **heteronomy** with English, which was formerly the national language of Scotland. The **dialect continuum** on which Scots was a **superposed variety** covers lowland southern and eastern Scotland but not the Highlands and Islands, which were until recently – and in some cases still are – Gaelic-speaking. These dialects are also known as Scots. In modern times some **autonomy** from English has been re-established, and many literary and other works have been published in Scots. See also **Ulster-Scots**. The literary form of the Scots language is often known as **Lallans**, and the Scots Language Society publishes a journal called *Lallans* of which it says:

> For ane an twintie year *Lallans*, the magazine o the Scots Leid Associe, haes featurt the bestest current writin in Scots, baith in poetry an prose. Writers o aa kynds haes kythed atween its batters. Thay'v shawn the ongaun virr an vitality o Scots as a leevin tung. Thare's nae wallaein in auld lang syne. *Lallans* in its editorial policy haes aye setten heich staundarts for Scots writin.

Scouse A popular name for the dialect and accent of the town of Liverpool, in northern England.

Sea Island Creole English see **Gullah**

secular linguistics A view of **sociolinguistics** as a methodology – a way of doing linguistics – associated particularly with the American linguist William Labov, and sometimes also known as quantitative sociolinguistics or, less properly, **correlational sociolinguistics**. Secular linguistics has as its objective a series of goals which are no different from those of any other sort of linguistics, but it works on the assumption that linguistic hypotheses and theories should be based on observations and analyses of **vernacular**

varieties as these are used by ordinary speakers (i.e. not by linguists) in everyday **social contexts**. The research of linguists working in their offices on their intuitions concerning their own dialect of their own language needs to be supplemented and checked by work on (usually tape-recorded samples of) real language in real contexts. One of the particular concerns of secular linguistics is the attempt to achieve an understanding of linguistic change, and much work in this field is devoted to studying linguistic changes in progress.

Séguy, Jean see **dialectometry**

self report tests Tests in which subjects are presented with a number of variants of a **linguistic variable** and asked to say which one of them they actually use in their own speech. This very often results in providing information about subjects' attitudes to these variants rather than about their actual usage. See **overreporting, underreporting.**

Selinker, Larry see **interlanguage**

semantics see **pragmatics**

semantic transparency A term used to refer to the phenomenon whereby the meaning of a word is apparent from the meaning of its component parts. Thus, the English word *dentist* is not semantically transparent, whereas the Norwegian word *tannlege*, literally 'tooth doctor', is. The term is often used in the discussion of **pidgin** languages, where the phenomenon occurs frequently. In a well-known example, **Tok Pisin** has *hosman* 'horse man' and *hosmeri* 'horse woman' corresponding to English *stallion* and *mare*.

semilingualism The discredited hypothesis that some children growing up in a bilingual environment may fail to learn either of the two languages fully, and may thus be 'doubly semilingual'. Very rarely, it can happen that in rather special bilingual situations a new language may be formed which is a mixture of the original two languages in roughly equal proportions – see **language intertwining** – but in this case the children who grow up speaking the new language have a fully-fledged language at their disposal and can in no sense be said to be 'semilingual'. See also **focused**.

Serbian see **Serbo-Croat**

Serbo-Croat A **polycentric standard** language from the **South Slavic dialect continuum** which was formally the major **official language** of Yugoslavia. It is now often considered to be three separate languages, although these are extremely similar and have total **mutual intelligibility**: Serbian (in Serbia, Montenegro and Bosnia), Croatian (in Croatia and Bosnia) and Bosnian (in Bosnia).

sex and language see **genderlect**

sharp stratification In Labovian **secular linguistics**, **linguistic variables** are employed to investigate **social stratification** and **style stratification**. This stratification can take the form of **fine stratification** or 'sharp stratification'. In sharp stratification, the correlation between social or stylistic factors and linguistic variables reveals a relatively uncontinuum-like situation, with sharp breaks in linguistic behaviour, and thus in percentages of variants of linguistic variables, between one social group or style and another.

Shelta An **antilanguage** vocabulary used by Travellers (but not by Romani) in Ireland and elsewhere in the British Isles, notably the Scottish Highlands, also known as 'Gammon'. It is derived for the most part from Irish Gaelic and includes **back slang** and other deliberate disguising devices. The vocabulary can be used within the context of either Gaelic or English grammar and phonology. Words which have passed from Shelta into English **slang** include *monicker* 'name' from Shelta *munnick* from Irish *ainm*; and *gammy* 'bad' from Shelta *gyamyath* from Irish *cam*.

signifying A speech act associated with speakers of **African American Vernacular English** in which criticism is directed at another person indirectly. See also **indirectness**, **speech act theory**.

simplification A process involved in both **pidginisation** and koinéisation, and occurring also in other forms of linguistic change. Simplification refers most importantly to an increase in regularity in a language variety, for example the regularisation of irregular verbs. It also refers to phenomena such as the loss of grammatical gender, the loss of case endings, and an increase in **semantic transparency**, such as the replacement of *optician* by *eye-doctor*.

slang Vocabulary which is associated with very informal or colloquial **styles**, such as English *batty* (mad) or *ace* (excellent). Some items of slang, like *ace*, may be only temporarily fashionable, and thus come to be associated with particular age-groups in a society. Other slang words and phrases may stay in the language for generations. Formerly slang vocabulary can acquire more formal stylistic status, such as modern French *tête* (head) from Latin *testa* (pot) and English *bus*, originally an abbreviation of *omnibus*. Slang should not be confused with **non-standard dialect**. (See also **style**.) Slang vocabulary in English has a number of different sources, including **Angloromani**, **Shelta** and **Yiddish**, together with devices such as **rhyming slang** and **back slang** as well as abbreviation (as in *bus*) and metaphor, such as *hot* meaning 'stolen' or 'attractive'.

social class dialect see **sociolect**

social context The totality of features in a social situation, involving location, participants and their relationships with each other, which may influence speakers' linguistic behaviour and which may, for example, lead to style shifting (see **style**). The 'study of language in its social context' is another way of referring to **secular linguistics**. The implication of this term is that it is important to study language as it is used by ordinary people in ordinary social situations, as well as or instead of the language of linguists, and language spoken in a laboratory. Secular linguistic research is thus based on the observing and recording of everyday speech rather than on the tapping of the linguist's intuitions about his or her own variety.

social dialect see **sociolect**

social dialect continuum see **dialect continuum**, **implicational scale**, **implicational table**

social dialectology see **dialectology**, **secular linguistics**, **urban dialectology**

social network An anthropological concept referring to the multiple web of relationships an individual contracts in a society with other people who he or she is bound to directly or indirectly by ties of friendship, kinship or other social relationships. This concept was introduced into sociolinguistic research by the British sociolinguists James Milroy and Lesley Milroy in connection with their research in Belfast. Lesley Milroy's book *Language and social networks* explains differential linguistic behaviour on the part of different social groups in terms of their different network structures and in particular in terms of **network strength**. See also **peer group**.

social psychology of language An area of the study of the relationship between language and society which examines **language attitudes** and looks at sociopsychological aspects of language use in **face-to-face interaction**, such as the extent to which speakers are able to manipulate situations by **code-switching**. An important tool in research in the social psychology of language is the **matched-guise technique**.

social stratification A term from sociology referring to a model of society in which a society is divided or ordered into horizontal 'layers' or 'strata', such as social classes or status groups, where people in the 'top' layers have more power, wealth and status than those in the 'bottom' layers. In **secular linguistics**, **linguistic variables** are said to be subject to social stratification if they correlate in some way with this social hierarchy. Social stratification is contrasted in secular linguistics with **style stratification**. See also **fine stratification, sharp stratification**.

sociolect A **variety** or **lect** which is thought of as being related to its speakers' social background rather than geographical background. A social class dialect is thus a form of sociolect. See also **acrolect, basilect** and **mesolect**.

sociolinguistics A term used to describe all areas of the study of the relationship between language and society other than those which are purely social scientific in their objectives, such as **ethnomethodology**. Sociolinguistic research is thus work which is intended to achieve a better understanding of the nature of human language by studying language in its **social context** and/or to achieve a better understanding of the nature of the relationship and interaction between language and society. Sociolinguistics includes **anthropological linguistics, dialectology, discourse analysis, ethnography of speaking, geolinguistics, language contact** studies, **secular linguistics,** the **social psychology of language** and the **sociology of language.**

sociolinguistic variable see **linguistic variable**

sociology of language A branch of **sociolinguistics** which deals on a large or **macrosociolinguistic** scale with issues relating to the relationship between sociological factors and language, and in particular with issues relating to language choice. It thus incorporates the study of topics such as **multilingualism, language planning, language maintenance** and **language shift.**

sociophonetics The sociolinguistic study of phonetic features and/or the use of phonetic techniques and expertise for carrying out sociolinguistic work.

Solomon Islands Pidgin see **Pijin**

sounding A form of **verbal duelling,** involving the exchange of ritual insults, associated with speakers of **African American Vernacular English,** especially young males.

source language In the study of **pidgin** and **creole** languages, the language from which a pidgin or creole is said to have derived, and which in particular has provided the bulk of its vocabulary. An English-based pidgin is thus a creole language which has resulted from large-scale **pidginisation** of English by non-native speakers in a **language contact** situation, and the vocabulary of which is largely English in origin. The source language is often also known as the target language, but this is a less desirable term since it implies that the speakers responsible for the pidginisation were actually attempting, unsuccessfully, to acquire the source language as such, which may well not have been the case.

South, The A geographical term used in American English dialectology. Confusingly, it does not refer to the whole of the southern United States but to the south-east. The core of the area, sometimes called the Deep South, is formed by the states of Louisiana, Alabama, Mississippi, Georgia and South Carolina, together with northern Florida (paradoxically, most of Florida, the southern-most state, is not part of The South), with the rest of the area being formed by North Carolina, Virginia, Tennessee, Arkansas, Kentucky, eastern Texas and West Virginia.

South Slavic dialect continuum A **dialect continuum** comprising the dialects of the South Slavic languages Slovenian, **Croatian, Bosnian, Serbian, Macedonian** and Bulgarian. The continuum ranges from eastern Italy and southern Austria through Slovenia, Croatia, Bosnia-Herzegovina, Yugoslavia (not including most of Kosovo), Macedonia and Bulgaria to northern Greece. A small area of northern Albania may also be included.

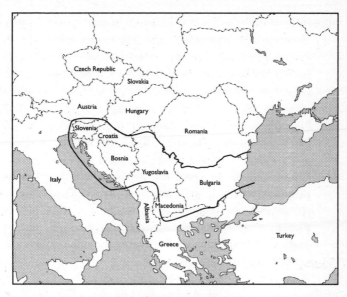

South Slavic dialect continuum

speech act A term used in **discourse analysis**, **ethnography of speaking** and **pragmatics** for the minimal unit of analysis of conversational interaction. A number of speech acts combine to form a **speech event**. Speech acts include greetings, summonses, jokes, commands, apologies and introductions.

speech act theory A theory associated with the work of the British philosopher J. L. Austin, in his 1962 book *How to do things with words*, which distinguishes between three facets of a **speech act**: the *locutionary act*, which has to do with the simple act of a speaker saying something; the *illocutionary act*, which has to do with the intention behind a speaker's saying something; and the *perlocutionary act*, which has to do with the actual effect produced by a speaker saying something. The *illocutionary force* of a speech act is the effect which a speech act is intended to have by the speaker.

speech community A community of speakers who share the same **verbal repertoire**, and who also share the same norms for linguistic behaviour, including both general norms for language use of the type studied in the **ethnography of speaking**, and more detailed norms for activities such as **style** shifting of the type studied by **secular linguistics**. It is an important term in both the ethnography of speaking and in secular linguistics.

speech event A higher level unit for the analysis of conversational interaction than the **speech act**. A speech event consists of one or more speech acts. The term is used in **discourse analysis**, **ethnography of speaking** and **pragmatics**. Examples of speech events include conversations, lectures and prayers.

spelling pronunciation A phenomenon due to a combination of literacy and **linguistic insecurity** in which the original pronunciation of a word is replaced by a newer pronunciation which more closely resembles the spelling. Twentieth-century spelling pronunciations which are now common in English include: *often* /oftn/, formerly /ofn/; *waistcoat* /weistkout/, formerly /wɛskit/; and *Ipswich* /ipswitʃ/, formerly /ipsidʒ/.

Sprachbund see **linguistic area**

Sranan A **creole** language with English as the **lexifier** which has more than 100,000 native speakers in coastal **Surinam**. The language is also known as 'Sranan Tongo' i.e. 'Surinam tongue'. It is used as a **lingua franca** by those members of the population of the country who do not speak it natively. It is distinct from but with a number of resemblances to **Ndjuka**. Sranan is a 'deep' creole, that is, because the official colonial language of the country was

Dutch, Sranan has been little influenced by English and, unlike in the case of **Jamaican Creole**, no **post-creole continuum** has developed. It has, however, borrowed a certain amount of lexis from Dutch. An idea of the distance between Sranan and English can be gained from the following:

Lek fa Luki ben gwenti, fos sabaten a b'e krin hen kruyara, bika te a b'e go na doro, te neti hen krosi no ben mu doti. Den yonkman ben sabi now bub-bun, san ben de fu du nanga den mati, namku sens a grandinari-brad ben ori wan langa taki naga hen.

'As was his custom, Luti cleaned his canoe in the early evening, because when he went out at night he did not want his clothes to be soiled. The boys knew full well what ailed their friend, especially since the elder of the church had chatted with him for a long time.'

The origins of many of these words in English is clear. For example:

krin < clean	doti < dirty
bika < because	taki < talk
neti < night	krosi < clothes
langa < long	hen < him

stabilisation A process whereby a formerly **diffuse** language variety that has been in a state of flux undergoes focusing (see **focused**) and takes on a more fixed and stable form that is shared by all its speakers. Pidginised **jargons** become **pidgins** through the process of stabilisation. **Dialect mixtures** may become **koinés** as a result of stabilisation. Stabilisation is also a component of language **standardisation**.

standard see **divergent dialect community, standardisation**

Standard English The **dialect** of English which is normally used in writing, is spoken by educated native speakers, and is taught to non-native speakers studying the language. There is no single **accent** associated with this dialect, but the lexicon and grammar of the dialect have been subject to **codification** in numerous dictionaries and grammars of the English language. Standard English is a **polycentric standard** variety, with English, Scottish, American, Australian and other standard varieties differing somewhat from one another. All other dialects can be referred to collectively as **nonstandard English**.

standardisation The process by which a particular variety of a language is subject to **language determination, codification** and **stabilisation**. These processes, which lead to the development of a standard language, may be the result of deliberate **language planning** activities, as with the standardisation of Indonesian, or not, as with the standardisation of English.

standard languages see **standardisation, koiné**

standard variety A variety of language which has undergone **standardisation** and which has acquired **autonomy**.

status planning In **language planning,** status planning refers to decisions which have to be taken concerning the selection of particular languages or varieties of language for particular purposes in the society or nation in question. Decisions about which language or languages are to be the national or official languages of particular nation-states are among the more important of status planning issues. Status planning is often contrasted with **corpus planning** or **language development**.

In the usage of most writers, status planning is not significantly different from **language determination**.

Steinsholt, Anders see **real-time studies, language missionary**

stereotype In **secular linguistics**, a **marker**, that is a **linguistic variable** which shows both **social stratification** and **style stratification**, which has attracted conscious attention and become the topic of overt comment. In investigations of the **embedding problem** associated with linguistic change, stereotypes represent a relatively late stage in the development of linguistic variables, having variants which have undergone extreme **stigmatisation**, and, as a result, having become involved in linguistic **change from above**.

stigmatisation Negative evaluation of linguistic forms. Work carried out in **secular linguistics** has shown that a linguistic change occurring in one of the lower **sociolects** in a **speech community** will often be negatively evaluated, because of its lack of association with higher status groups in the community, and the form resulting from the change will therefore come to be regarded as 'bad' or 'not correct'. Stigmatisation may subsequently lead to **change from above**, and the development of the form into a **marker** and possibly, eventually, into a **stereotype**.

Strine A journalistic term for Australian English, supposedly derived from the Australian way of pronouncing 'Australian'.

style In **sociolinguistics**, a **variety** of a **language** which is associated with **social context** and which differs from other styles in terms of their formality. Styles can thus be ranged on a continuum from very formal to highly informal or colloquial. In English, stylistic differentiation is most often signalled by lexical differences. Thus, in British English, *to slumber*, *to sleep* and *to kip* all mean the same thing, but are stylistically different. Styles are in principle distinct from **dialects** and from **registers**: non-standard dialect speakers can and do employ formal styles, and standard speakers can and do use informal styles. Highly informal vocabulary is often referred to as **slang.** Changing from one style to another – or, better, moving along the continuum of styles – as the formality of a situation changes, or in order to change the formality of a situation, is known as style shifting.

style shifting see **style**

style axiom An axiom adumbrated by Allan Bell in connection with **stylistic variation** in language which claims that variation on the style dimension within the speech of a single speaker derives from and echoes the variation which exists between speakers on the social dimension.

style stratification A term from **secular linguistics** which refers to the correlation of **linguistic variables** with **social context** and formality. A variable which is subject to style stratification in a speech community will show different use of different **variants** in different social situations. Thus, in many forms of British English, the [ʔ] variant of the variable (t) – the pronunciation of /t/ in words such as *bet* and *better* as a **glottal stop** – occurs more frequently in informal than in formal styles. Variables which are subject to style stratification are known as **markers.**

stylistic variation see **style**

subjective reaction tests Tests, including the use of the **matched guise technique** and other techniques, in which subjects are asked to evaluate speakers on the basis of recordings of their speech.

submersion An educational practice in which individual children are placed in a school where the teachers and other pupils do not speak their native language, often an **immigrant language**. Compare **immersion programme**.

substratum A substratum effect is one which results **diachronically** from the process of **language shift** in which a community, in abandoning its native language for another language which has been imposed on it from above i.e. by another more powerful community, carries over features from its original language, through the process of **admixture**, into the new language. Irish English, for example, is often said to demonstrate substratum effects from Irish Gaelic. The sociolinguistic opposite of substratum is *superstratum*, where it is a more powerful group that experiences language shift, as when the Germanic-speaking Frankish overlords of northern France abandoned their Germanic speech, but not without leaving behind many traces of this in modern French. The term *adstratum* is generally used to refer to situations where two groups of roughly equal status come into contact with one another and exert mutual influence on one another's languages without language shift taking place. The result of this process is known as a **linguistic area**.

superposed variety A **variety** which is 'placed above' a geographical dialect continuum in the sense that it has a social function of some kind over a wider geographical area than any of the continuum's constituent dialects. Most often, superposed varieties are **standard varieties** with the characteristic of **autonomy**. **Roofless dialects** are dialects above which there has been raised no autonomous superposed variety.

superstratum see **substratum**

Surinam A nation state in northern South America, formerly the Dutch colony Dutch Guiana, well-known in **sociolinguistics** as the home of the **creole** languages **Ndjuka, Saramakkan and Sranan.**

synchronic see **diachronic**

T

T and V pronouns A distinction made by many languages of the world between familiar forms of the second-person pronouns (corresponding to English *you*) and polite or formal forms. In **sociolinguistics**, these are known as T and V pronouns respectively, after the first letter of the familiar and polite forms in French, *tu* and *vous*. Most often, T forms are used as **address forms** for close friends and family members, while V forms are used to address strangers and other less intimate acquaintances, but there are also numerous differences between languages and dialects. In some languages, the V form was originally a second-person plural form, as in French. In others, as in the case of German *Sie* (as opposed to familiar *du*), it was originally a third person plural form. Other examples from European languages include:

	T	V
Greek	esi	esis
Norwegian	du	De
Swedish	du	Ni
Welsh	ti	chwi
Romansh	ti	vus
Slovenian	ti	vi

taboo Behaviour which is believed to be supernaturally forbidden and/or highly immoral and/or very improper, and which is prohibited for irrational rather than rational reasons. Originally from a word found in the Polynesian languages with the form *tapu* or similar. Language taboo has to do with words and expressions which are supposed not to be used, and which are shocking, offensive, blasphemous or indecent when they are used. In **anthropological linguistics**, the study of linguistic taboo is of interest for what it tells us about the moral, religious and other values of a community. 'Swear words' are common examples of words which are subject to linguistic taboo.

talk see **ethnomethodology**

target language The language which a non-native learner is trying to learn. See also **source language**.

t,d-deletion A variable phenomenon in the phonology of English whereby word-final /t/ and /d/ in words like *west*, *missed*, *hold*, *rolled* are not pronounced, especially if the next word begins with another consonant. Some dialects delete more than others, and there is a tendency for /t/ and /d/ to be dropped less where they are a marker of the past tense, as in *missed*, than where they are not, as in *mist*. See **constraints**.

text linguistics see **discourse analysis**

t-glottaling A feature of many English accents in which **intervocalic** and word-final /t/, as in *better*, *bet*, are pronounced as a **glottal stop**.

th-fronting A feature of some English accents, notably **Cock-ney**, in which the interdental fricative consonants /θ/ and /ð/, both written *th*, have as a result of a sound-change come to be pronounced as the corresponding labio-dental fricatives /f/ and /v/, so that *thin* is pronounced the same as *fin*, and *loathes* is pronounced the same as *loaves*. The name comes from the fact that /f/ and /v/ are pronounced further towards the front of the vocal tract than the two *th* sounds.

Tok Pisin Originally an English-**lexifier pidgin** language, now a creole spoken by about 50,000 native speakers in Papua New Guinea. The name of the language means, literally, 'pidgin talk'. It is also very widely used in the country as a second language **lingua franca**, and plays an important role in the parliament and media. It is related to and rather similar to **Bislama** and **Pijin**. The following is part of a story in Tok Pisin taken from the Papua New Guinea newspaper *Wantok*:

Long pasis bilong Kandrian long Wes Nu Briten i gat tripela naispela ailan i sanap long wanpela lain tasol. Tripela i wanmak na antap bilong wan wan i stret olsem ples balus. I luk olsem bipo ol i wanpela tasol, na wanpela samting i bin katim tripela hap. Na tru tumas, ol lapun i stori olsem. Wanpela bikman bilong ples ol i kolim Ais i sindaun stori long *Wantok* ripota i raun long dispela hap. Na wanpela lapun meri tu i sindaun long dua bilong haus bilong em long nambis na i stori tu.

By the shores of Kandrian in West New Britain, there are three nice islands that stand in a row. The three islands are the same size. Each is flat on top like an airfield. Before, they did not look like this. There was just one island and something divided it into three pieces. This is the truth. The old people tell the story like this. A leader from a place called Ais sat down and told the story to a *Wantok* Newspaper reporter about this place. An old woman sat at the door of her house by the beach and told it too.

topic see **domain**

trade language A **lingua franca** which is used mainly for informal commercial purposes.

traditional dialect An English term corresponding to German *Mundart* and French **patois** which refers to dialects which have been relatively unaffected by koinéisation and/or by **dialect contact** with the **standard variety**. In the English-speaking world, traditional dialects are found only in England, northern Ireland, the Lowlands of Scotland, and Newfoundland. Some dialectologists would also include the American dialects of the **Ozarks** and the **Applachians** under this heading. They are linguistically conservative, compared to other dialects, and diverge linguistically from one another and the standard variety quite considerably. They are also associated particularly but not exclusively with the speech of **NORMS**. In England, pronunciations of a word such as *bone* as [bien], [ben] or [bwun] are typical of traditional dialects. Pronunciations typical of non-traditional or modern dialects include [boun], [bo:n] and [bæun].

traditional dialectology The study of **traditional dialects** using the traditional methods of **dialectology**. The term can also be applied to research into urban and other non-traditional dialects involving the use of only older-style, that is, non-**secular-linguistic**, methodology. The concepts of **iso-**

gloss, **focal area** and **transition zone** are due to work in traditional dialectology.

transfer see **admixture**

transition zone A concept from **traditional dialectology** and more recent work in **dialectometry, geolinguistics** (1) and spatial **dialectology**. Traditional dialectologists discovered early on in the history of the discipline that **isoglosses** for individual words and pronunciations rarely coincided with each other. One reaction to that finding was to suggest that there was no such thing as a dialect totally distinct from other dialects. This is, in most cases, strictly-speaking correct (see **dialect continuum**), but it is not simply the case that isoglosses are randomly distributed. Dialect features show different types of geographical patterning. Some geographical areas are crossed by no or relatively few isoglosses. These are **focal areas**. Focal areas are surrounded by transition zones which separate them from other focal areas. Transition zones are crossed by relatively large numbers of isoglosses, sometimes called bundles of isoglosses, few of them taking exactly the same course, but often running in roughly the same direction, depending on how far and in what direction innovations have spread outwards from the focal area. The transition from one 'dialect' (or better, dialect area) to another thus appears to be gradual rather than abrupt.

transparency see **morphological transparency, semantic transparency**

Tristan da Cunha An English-speaking South Atlantic British dependent territory which consists of six small islands about halfway between southern Africa and South America. The only populated island, Tristan da Cunha, has a population of about 290. It is said to be the most remote permanently inhabited settlement in the world, the nearest habitation being **St Helena**, which is about 1,200 miles away. A British garrison was stationed on the hitherto uninhabited Tristan da Cunha in 1816, as a result of fears that it might be used as a base for an attempt to rescue Napoleon from St Helena. When the garrison left in 1817, three soldiers asked to stay, and during the 1800s they were joined by shipwrecked sailors, a few European settlers, and six women from St Helena. By 1886 the population was ninety-seven. In 1961 a volcanic eruption threatened the settlement, and the inhabitants were evacuated to England. Most of them returned to Tristan in 1963. The English is remarkable. It is mainly of English dialect origin but shows some signs of **pidginisation**, though probably not enough to be considered a **creoloid**. It has a number of grammatical features found nowhere else in the anglophone world, such as double past tense marking, as in *we used to went*.

turn-taking A term from **conversation analysis** used to describe the basic mechanism on which conversation is based. In a conversation, each speaker is entitled to 'turns', where a turn is his or her right and obligation to speak. Conversation is organised in such a way that only one speaker speaks at any one time, and changes of speaker occur. If speaker change does not occur, what results is a monologue, not a conversation. Turn-taking is thus an essential component of conversation.

U

Überdachung see **roofless dialects**

Ulster-Scots The dialects spoken in the far north and northeast of Ireland which are descended from dialects of **Scots**.

The standard language, sometimes called *Ullans*, which corresponds to these dialects, and which does have a history of use as a written language, is regarded by its supporters as a language distinct from, though related to, **Lallans**. Part of the gospel of St Matthew, in a modern Ulster-Scots translation, is as follows:

> Jesus wuz boarn in thà toon o Bethlehem in Judea, in thà day of Käng Herod. It wuz nae time ava eftèr this afore a wheen spaemen fae tha Aist cum til Jerusalem an begoud speirin, 'Quhar wud thà bairn be at bees tae be tha Käng o tha Jews? We hae saen hìs starn ris up in thà Aist, an haes cum for tae warschip hìm'.

urban dialectology The study of **dialects** spoken in urban areas. This is sometimes contrasted with **traditional dialectology**, but urban dialects can also of course be studied using 'traditional' methods. Urban dialectology was also used as a term in the 1960s to refer to what is now called **secular linguistics**, but this usage is now inappropriate in view of the use of secular linguistic methods to study many other kinds of language **variety** than urban dialects.

underreporting A term used, in connection with **self report tests**, to describe claims by respondents that they use lower status or more nonstandard linguistic forms than they actually do use, thus revealing favourable attitudes to such forms. In tests involving English speakers, male respondents have been statistically more likely to report in this way than female respondents.

Vanuatu see **Bislama**

Varbrul A computer program developed by the Montreal-based linguists Henrietta Cedergren and David Sankoff for the analysis of large amounts of data on **linguistic variables** obtained by **secular linguistic** research, and the development from this data of **variable rules**. This program greatly facilitates and speeds up the analysis of the differential effects of particular **constraints** on the selection of particular **variants** of a variable.

variable see **linguistic variable**

variable rule A concept introduced by the American linguist William Labov as a result of one of the major findings of secular linguistic research, namely that much variation in language is constrained by linguistic factors in a probabilistic kind of way which cannot adequately be represented as resulting from optional rules, since the rules are not truly 'optional' at all. Thus, the **t-glottaling** rule /t/→ [ʔ]/V—, which produces pronunciations such as *better* [bɛʔə] and *bet* [bɛʔ] in many forms of British English, is not obligatory because pronunciations such as [bɛtə] and [bɛt] also occur. Neither, however, is it truly optional, since the frequency with which the rule operates is influenced by a number of **constraints**, such as whether the /t/ is or is not word-final, and whether or not the /t/ is followed by a vowel, which combine to influence the probability that the rule will apply.

variant see **linguistic variable**

variation theory see **linguistic variation and change**

variational linguistics see **linguistic variation and change**

variety A neutral term used to refer to any kind of language – a **dialect**, **accent**, **sociolect**, **style** or **register** – that a linguist happens to want to discuss as a separate entity for some particular purpose. Such a variety can be very general, such as 'American English', or very specific, such as 'the lower working-class dialect of the Lower East Side of New York City'. See also **lect**.

verbal deprivation A now totally discredited notion developed by certain American educational psychologists in the 1970s, sometimes referred to as 'language deficit'. They argued that certain (mostly African American) lower-class speakers of American English either (a) spoke dialects that were in themselves inadequate for the expression of abstract concepts and logical relationships, and/or (b) had not acquired enough of their native dialect to carry out such tasks, because of insufficient verbal stimulation. American linguists, led by William Labov, were able to show that the educational psychologists were arguing from a position based on (a) ignorance of the grammatical structure of English dialects and (b) ignorance of **secular linguistic** methodology and of problems of research in this area, notably that concerning the **observer's paradox**. Some writers mistakenly identified verbal deprivation with Bernstein's **restricted code**.

verbal duelling A **speech event** found in many cultures in which speakers, most often children and adolescents, compete playfully with each other verbally in various ways including, for example, through the exchange of ritual insults i.e. insults which adhere to a set formula and are not intended to be taken seriously.

verbal repertoire A term which refers to the totality of language varieties available to a **speech community**. Such repertoires will include different **styles**, and may also include different dialects in bidialectal or diglossic communities, and, in multilingual communities, different languages. Communities may reveal the range of their verbal repertoires through **code-switching**.

vernacular variety The indigenous **language** variety of a particular **speech community**. The term is used particularly to refer to dialects which are not national languages or **standard varieties** or **lingua francas**; to **nonstandard dialects** which have not been influenced by standard varieties; and to **styles** which are closely associated with informal contexts. In the **sociology of language**, vernacular languages are a focus of **language planning** debates about the extent to which education should be carried on through the medium of the mother tongue rather than the national language or languages. In **secular linguistics**, vernacular varieties are thought to be the most desirable object of study, being most regular and systematic because they have been least influenced by other varieties and by notions of **correctness**.

vitality A term used in the **sociology of language** for establishing a typology of language varieties. A **language** which has a community of native speakers is said to have the characteristic of vitality. **Varieties** which are undergoing **language shift** or **language death** have less vitality than other language varieties. **Classical languages** such as Latin and Sanskrit, which no longer have native speakers, and **pidgin** languages, which do not (yet) have native speakers, do not have the characteristic of vitality.

Vlach Varieties of Eastern Romance spoken in the southern Balkans are referred to by linguists as *Arumanian*. Speakers of these varieties are known as *Vlachs*, and their language, by non-linguists, as Vlach. From a sociolinguistic point of view, there is the interesting **Ausbau** sociolinguistic problem of whether Vlach is a dialect of Rumanian or not. This linguistic problem naturally has parallels with the ethnic question of whether Vlachs are 'really' Romanians or not. Mutual intelligibility between Vlach and Rumanian is not always easy because of the rather large degree of **Abstand**. The Greek practice of referring to Balkan Romance as it is spoken in Greece as *Vlachika* has the effect of implying that the language is not Romanian, and that the people are therefore not Romanian either.

W

Weinreich, Uriel see **compound bilingualism, coordinate bilingualism, diasystem**

West Germanic dialect continuum A **dialect continuum** comprising the dialects of Frisian, Dutch, Luxemburgish and German. The area covers the whole of the Netherlands and Luxemburg, northern and eastern Belgium, parts of north-

West Germanic dialect continuum

eastern and eastern France, central and eastern Switzerland, and almost all of Austria. It also extends into northern Italy, southern Denmark and western Poland.

West Romance dialect continuum A **dialect continuum** comprising the dialects of French, **Franco-Provençal, Occitan,** Catalan, Spanish, **Galician,** Portuguese, Italian, **Ladin, Friulian** and **Romansh.** The area covers Portugal, all of Spain except the Basque-speaking area, most of France, southern Belgium, western and southern Switzerland, and almost all of Italy. In the Iberian peninsula, the continuum is most apparent in the north. Because of settlement patterns involving north-to-south movement following the reconquest of the southern part of the peninsula from the Moors, the breaks between Portuguese and Spanish, and Spanish and Catalan, are sharper in the south.

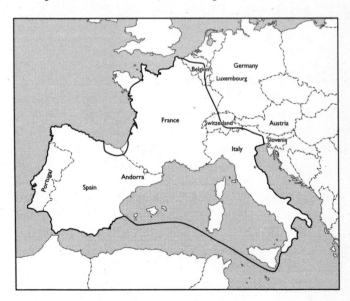

West Romance dialect continuum

Wolfram, Walt see **linguistic gratuity, principle of**

Y

Yiddish A language, sometimes known as Judaeo-German, which is spoken by Jewish people in many parts of the world. Most speakers today speak Eastern Yiddish, which developed in eastern Europe and therefore contains many words of Slavic (especially Polish, Russian and Ukrainian) origin. Yiddish grew out of mediaeval German Rhineland dialects and is essentially still a form of German, but it has a number of archaisms and independent innovations. As with **Ladino,** the Jewish cultural and religious vocabulary is derived from Hebrew. Yiddish is normally written in the Hebrew alphabet. Yiddish has been a frequent source of words in English **slang,** such as British English *nosh* 'food' and American English *shlep* 'drag'.

Z

Zulu pidgin see **Fanakaló**

Sources

I owe the Angloromany text to Ian Hancock.

The Bislama text is taken from *Gud nyus bilong Jisas Krais: the four gospels in New Hebrides Bislama* (1971).

The Nynorsk version of the Norwegian example in the Bokmål entry is taken from J. T. Faarlund 'Norma in nynorsk sedd i høve til austlandsmåla' in T. Kleiva, I. Donali, T. Nesset and H. Øygarden (eds) *Austlandsmål i endring* (Oslo: Det Norske Samlaget, 1999). The Bokmål 'translation' is my own.

The Franco-Provençal examples are based on A. Martinet *La description phonologique avec application au parler franco-provençal d'Hauteville (Savoie)* (Geneva: Librairie Droz, 1956).

The Kriol text is taken from *Brom top im album yu* (New Paris, IN: World Missionary Press).

The Occitan examples are taken from D. Ager *Sociolinguistics and contemporary French* (Cambridge: Cambridge University Press, 1990).

The Russenorsk sentence is quoted from Ernst Håkon Jahr 'On the pidgin status of Russenorsk' in E. H. Jahr and I. Broch (eds) *Language contact in the Arctic: northern pidgins and contact languages* (Berlin: Mouton de Gruyter, 1996).

The Sranan text is taken from the work of Trefossa, the pseudonym of Henny de Ziel, published in J. Voorhoeve and U. M. Lichtfeld *Creole drum: an anthology of creole literature in Surinam* (New Haven: Yale University Press, 1975).

The Ulster-Scots example is taken from P. Robinson *Ulster-Scots: a grammar of the traditional written and spoken language* (Belfast: Ullans Press, 1997).

BIBLIOGRAPHY

Chambers, J. K. (1995) *Sociolinguistic theory*, Oxford: Blackwell.

Chambers, J. K. and Peter Trudgill (1998) *Dialectology* (2nd edn), Cambridge: Cambridge University Press.

Chambers, J. K., Peter Trudgill and Natalie Schilling-Estes (eds) (2002) *The handbook of language variation and change*, Oxford: Blackwell.

Cheshire, Jenny and Peter Trudgill (eds) (1998) *The sociolinguistics reader, vol. 2: Gender and discourse*, London: Arnold.

Coates, J. (ed.) (1998) *Language and gender: a reader*, Oxford: Blackwell.

Coulmas, Florian (ed.) (1997) *The handbook of sociolinguistics*, Oxford: Blackwell.

Coupland, Nikolas, and Adam Jaworski (eds) (1997) *Sociolinguistics: a reader*, London: Macmillan.

Downes, William (1998) *Language and society*, Cambridge: Cambridge University Press.

Fasold, Ralph (1984) *The sociolinguistics of society*, Oxford: Blackwell.

Fasold, Ralph (1990) *The sociolinguistics of language*, Oxford: Blackwell.

Foley, William (1997) *Anthropological linguistics: an introduction*, Oxford: Basil Blackwell.

Hoffman, Charlotte (1991) *An introduction to bilingualism*, London: Longman.

Holmes, Janet (1992) *An introduction to sociolinguistics*, London: Longman.

Hudson, Richard (1996) *Sociolinguistics* (2nd edn), Cambridge: Cambridge University Press.

Jaworsky, Adam and Nikolas Coupland (eds) (1999) *The discourse reader*, London: Routledge.

Johnstone, Barbara (2002) *Discourse Analysis*, Oxford: Blackwell.

Mesthrie, R., J. Swann, A. Deumert and W. L. Leap (2000) *Introducing sociolinguistics*, Edinburgh: Edinburgh University Press.

Romaine, Suzanne (1994) *Language in society: an introduction to sociolinguistics*, Oxford: Oxford University Press.